Source

(in-/out-/near-)

Patrick Ward

Thought Leader Press

Source

Copyright © 2023, Patrick Ward

Published by Thought Leader Press

New York/Oklahoma

Hardcover ISBN: 978-1-61343-153-5

Paperback ISBN: 978-1-61343-154-2

EBook ISBN: 978-1-61343-155-9

Table of Contents

Introduction

I would like to begin by saying that there are too many people who have gotten used to not only the way that we live currently but, more importantly (within this book's context), the way that we do business.

But first, a little about me.

At this point in my career, I have found myself not just in an industry, but in a veritable sea of people that does incredibly vital work today.

Most of the work done in the outsourcing space and the software development space is very mission-critical to how humans live their lives. Yet, it is a space that very few people know about, down to the most mundane, and besides people inside this industry, very few people understand what I do.

I am sure you know that the work that is done in this industry aligns with the philosophy of 'the businesses.' Ironically, those that are the most successful and make the most money are often very functional businesses that just sort of power our human civilization, rather than the 'sexy industries' that people are always talking about.

I felt that there was always a level of toxicity in how my industry was talked about within various spaces.

That's sort of the biggest thing that I'm trying to disrupt. As someone who has uniquely gone through so many different interactions with different cultures, I think that, again, another sort of very mundane principle, all humans are basically the same.

I get a lot of joy when I interact with people when I'm overseas. You realize, 'hey, these people have the same hopes and dreams, they have the same mindset.' They might even have the same family quirks, things that are just really elemental to humanity. I think what ends up unfortunately happening within our space and how conversations in business generally go, is that the humanity of people is really stripped away. We end up talking in terms of even calling people 'resources.' Our space ends up talking about people in dehumanizing ways. In many ways, it's just become a new wave of colonialism.

You see this all the time, particularly in the first wave of outsourcing with call centers. What I didn't like about that initial iteration of call centers and even the early phase of IT outsourcing to countries like India, is that businesses deliberately put it all in terms of cost, without factoring in the humans behind it.

There was always this superiority complex. It wasn't even just America who did this, you saw this in England as well. England had a similar perception of onshore, versus Poland for example, being offshore.

What I felt through all of that is we were once again entrenching a phenomenon that existed since the 1800s when Britain did its imperial conquest, and the other European powers did the same, entrenching a philosophy that even dates back to the Roman era.

I just feel like we, as a species, given that we have this collective shared humanity, can be better than that.

I look back to one of the promises of the Internet, that it was meant to bring us together. Yet, for a variety of reasons, it has cemented us into our different camps even more. Through this book, I would like to articulate a vision for the world, that we can still get back to that promise of what was said the Internet could do for society and bring in more understanding.

We can bring in a, 'the tide raises all boats' type of philosophy. Everyone can benefit as a result of this, and we can start to live in a truly connected world, reaping all the benefits that flow from it: less conflict and more prosperity for people. A real level up for our species.

I'm not saying it's going to be easy, which is why I think this book is for two different audiences. Given that this is still a business-oriented book, it does make sense that the primary audience is targeted towards the business owner and the executive. It's to help them understand that I believe this wave of prosperity is inevitable. Therefore, they should see some of the forerunner examples that they could adopt, but also that they should want to be on that train early.

Similarly, I would say there's a secondary audience, which is the wider business community at large, so employees can understand their part in the value chain. What ends up happening often is that outsourcing comes in and, as I mentioned about the conversation of cost, you start to get this idea of 'okay, do we go with labor? Do we go with capital? Do we start looking at AI to do something?'

You're basically pitting different parts of the business against each other. As any sound business-minded person would tell you, and I'm sure you guys would agree, you end up creating a toxic work environment that's non-beneficial for all as soon as you start creating a level of tension in your business where people can't be psychologically safe and can't do their best work.

While I still certainly want to be pragmatic with this, because I'm recognizing there's some sort of limitations–I'm not going to change the world with one book–but I certainly don't want an audience getting to the end of this book thinking, 'so what?'

With my speaking, my goal is always that whenever I get on stage and give a speech, I abide by the simple rule of three. Remembering that people are only going to remember three things once I come off that stage after 45 minutes, I want those three things to always be super actionable for my audience so they can use something from my speech to improve their lives.

I've always done that because I've been very contrarian to the usual crowd of speakers who are the Mark Cubans of the world, the Elon Musks of the world, the people who headline conferences, who basically say the usual bullshit platitudes.

Sure, they can get on stage, because they have been very successful. I'm not disputing the wisdom of what they say, but when someone like that gets on stage and says, "be yourself," and everyone cheers wildly, it might make you feel good in the moment, but then as soon as that person leaves the stage, the audience is left with, 'what can I do today to improve my life?'

That's where I'm still leaning this book, because while I want it to still speak to some of the fundamental truths that I believe do exist, I'm also not going to be upset if this book ends up dated in three to five years from now.

A couple of nights ago, I recently read through a chapter that I wrote years previously. I was horrendously embarrassed about what I wrote there, but I wasn't mad about it because it just showed me that the Patrick who wrote it from that year is a different person.

It once again reiterated some of these same themes. I have been able to improve myself, in no uncertain terms, because of my industry. I am an Australian living in America, working with Argentinians, Portuguese, Filipinos, Indians, people from right across the gamut of life experience.

I think there's something unique about both this space, and also more importantly this model. When you look at this sort of more ethereal goal, something that the UN has basically talked about since World War II ended, it's about cross-cultural communication. How do we bring people together?

And specifically, they were always targeting the younger generations because of the philosophy that "the younger generations are our future." How can we bring young people together to make sure that something like World War II never happens again?

I would argue that a lot of that can be seen through a microcosm of our industry. It might seem a little bit of a stretch, but I would argue that when you put people from completely disparate backgrounds trying to reach a common goal together, that's where you have those cultural sharings between one another.

That's when you start to dawn on that idea of, 'hey, we're not all that different.' It's a fairly simple idea. I know plenty of people have articulated it, but the fact that few people really embrace the idea of being a global citizen still surprises me to this day. It's about being part of one species as opposed to "but I'm still American," "I'm still Australian," "I'm still English," and even further subdivided, "I'm from this city or this town or this village." "I don't like those guys, they're over there, they're different from us."

I think of why this particularly matters to me. It really came back to one of my first experiences with a very different culture.

I joined an organization called AIESEC. Funnily enough, it was founded by the United Nations right after World War II to advance the goal that I've been talking about. That was when I did English and entrepreneurship teaching in Vietnam.

I think what was interesting about that experience is there is very little English, even to this day, in the country. It was the first place that forced me to learn a pretty substantial amount of the local language, at which I know Europeans are laughing at me, thinking like, 'well, we learned four to five languages since we're a child.' But it's a little rarer for an Australian.

What was particularly interesting about that experience is that this was 2012. I was still a relatively young man, in my late teens to early twenties, but it really thrust a lot of these ideas into my head. I was very acutely aware when I started on that program that I didn't want to be part of any "voluntourism (a trend where tourists travel somewhere and contribute to a charitable project)."

I didn't want it to be colonialistic or imperialistic. I wanted to make sure that the skills gap I was providing for was not something that already could be done by a local. I wasn't going to go and build an orphanage that was going to be torn down, only to be rebuilt by the next batch of young, dumb, white college kids later on.

With that experience, the reason I was aware that what I was doing was making somewhat of a difference, was because they don't have a lot of local English speakers. The reason that English teaching was tied with entrepreneurship was really important. It was because trade was the fastest growing industry in Vietnam, and the way that people were getting into that industry of trade was through being able to speak English and starting to deal with importing and exporting. This was substantially raising living conditions for each of those people in their towns and their communities.

They were starting to see the benefits of participating in this globalized world. I saw in that, once again, this microcosm that reveals itself when you don't lean into the traditional paternalistic values of colonialism and when you actually just engage with people like, "what can I do best, what can you do best, and we can prosper together." You're able to start realizing some of that promise: together, we can achieve an outcome that doesn't have to be "I win, you lose."

Because, ultimately, when you look at the way that money flows, it flows to those who provide a unique value in the marketplace. I would argue that every single human has a certain strain of expertise they uniquely know that no one else does, and it's key for each of us as individuals to discover what that unique expertise is.

I think many industries are deceptive in how they yield that expertise.

I think software development and outsourcing in general has been the closest we've gotten, and probably continues to be the closest we'll get, to actually realizing that promise of allowing people to do exactly the best work they are meant to be doing.

When you look at other industries that exist, they lean towards things like conformity. Being here in LA, one only has to look at the entertainment industry. The entertainment industry looks at pulling people in from disparate backgrounds, mining their creativity like a commodity, and is more than willing to spit them out when they no longer serve its needs.

By contrast, you look at tenures that people can earn. I always get particularly inspired when I meet people who were the early guys at IBM, for example. They're still in our space even to this day because there's something implicitly true about being a part of functions, structures, markets, and economies that ultimately power how our civilization functions, as opposed to being just the latest hot thing.

I think this is a continuation of the kick in the ass that the pandemic gave. But I think what I've seen and what I've been 'disappointed' by, which probably is a very strong impetus, comes back to this idea of remote versus in-person.

I think when the pandemic started, there was this idea that people were starting to open their minds to the concept of how they didn't have to be location dependent, or more importantly, they didn't have to be culture dependent. That was very encouraging.

Unfortunately, what we saw right after that is a regression. This is not just in our sector, but more broadly speaking, this idea that life could return to normal once the pandemic was "over."

I think what the world needs is, and I hesitate to use these types of phrases, and I certainly wouldn't want to articulate them in this way forever, but they need to embrace one of those early concepts of the pandemic: the idea of a 'new normal.'

Let's be more specific. Organizations need to embrace a world in which business can be conducted in a completely different way to how it was in the past.

The reason they need to do this is because you look at the types of companies who are forcing folks to go back to the office. You can already see this phenomenon starting to happen right now. By forcing people back to the office, they're likely doing it because of the fears of a recessionary environment and feeling like they can strongarm their employees into being at their beck and call.

What I see within that mindset is that it's still treating your people combatively, and it also has a knock-on effect. It means that the people who have the resources available to stay in big cities, to come into the office, who don't have family members they're trying to look after, who aren't in a particular location, those people who have slightly different circumstances but bring a lot of diversity, creativity, and innovation to organizations–suddenly they're being left behind.

What I don't like about that mindset is that it's a model that I fear tends to lean towards groupthink. It's a model that also is very short-term oriented. I understand that this is a classic problem that most corporations face, but I would argue that the aspiring entrepreneur or the corporate executive who doesn't want to just think about the next quarter, but actually wants to think about the longevity of the business they operate in, needs to embrace a truly globalized way of working. It's not just about being globalized because plenty of companies, like Delta, for example, are globalized with their call center in the Philippines, but they're not treating those posts very well.

It's more about the shift to understanding that when you create a distributed model in the right way, you build more prosperity, more resilience, and more value into your business. That's why I think it should matter to an executive.

As much as I can talk about some of the broader aspects that I think will be better for humanity, I still do genuinely believe in the business thesis that building distributed models where you are getting the best possible talent for every single function of your business means that you are earning a higher revenue per employee. And through earning that higher revenue per employee, you are going to achieve higher business multiples.

Now, is that a valuation that matters to you for an exit or a valuation that matters to you, even just in terms of ongoing revenue? Maybe this is a lifestyle business for an entrepreneur; maybe they're looking for a legacy play that could last for generations to come. If they're thinking in those terms, then they have to get away from this idea of 'we are located in this city or this town.'

Humanity is going to continue to advance. There's no city on earth that has access to all of the talent, all of the creativity, and all of the innovation. There's no organization that couldn't get better by adopting a distributed company structure.

This is not to say it's easy. This is something that is very clearly evident. You might have seen this with a layer of managers that weren't comfortable managing their teams in that structure. And there have been many publicized examples of things that have gone wrong. One only has to look at IBM. They went fully remote during the early 2000s and then brought people back to the office. There are also companies that have tried it and have failed to fully adopt the model in the right way.

I think there is still a way to do it, but I think that this comes back to the audience. The audience needs to grapple with this concept if they're going to create truly sustainable, successful, and long-term businesses.

I'm inviting you to disrupt everything you've ever known about how to set up a business.

I think this has been one core problem with most of the business executives I've encountered. They tend to lean towards both financial and corporate structure models that are cemented in the past. If they could, just for a moment, conceptualize a new way of forming their business, oriented around talent from "wherever." A model that didn't rely on even 50% in-person collaboration or above.

If they can disrupt that thinking, they are going to earn many times over the revenue they possibly could have imagined, because by cementing themselves in this new way, they are likely to do business in a way that will be beneficial for them and their employees and ultimately, be better suited to navigating any challenges that come.

Let me backtrack a little here.

The pandemic was not the first disruption we are going to face in our lifetime. A lot of business executives I speak to, talk about how the pandemic was hard. They talk about 2022 being hard. I'm sure they need to realize that there isn't going to be a return to "the good times of the early 2000s," or even "the good times of the mid-2010s." When I speak to older executives, they say, "the good times of the 1980s." We're not going back to that world.

We are only going to get more and more disruptions over the course of our lifetimes. Whether it's more war, another global pandemic or epidemic, or natural disasters. These disruptions are going to continue to happen. I don't see a way that life returns to this calm, peaceful vision, and therefore business returns to this calm, peaceful vision that many executives have been accustomed to.

You can either keep building your businesses in a way that will be subject to those disruptions, or you can build some innate resilience. You will weather any storm, regardless of what that storm may be, if you build some innate resilience with this type of model. That's really the key, because this harkening for nostalgia is something I've seen in all sorts of ways. I've heard it from SaaS executives who wish it was the fundraising era of the early 2010s. I've spoken with finance people who wish it was the deregulation era of the 1980s. I'm not saying we can't all feel the pinch of nostalgia from time to time, but to dwell in it is a fallacy.

That is not going to support you in achieving your business's goals. It's not going to get you the lifestyle and the impact you want to make on this world.

If you're trying to go back to that model, the model won't exist.

The reason you need to act now is because this is the pivotal point. We've just all collectively, as a species, come out of a once-in-a-hundred-years, generation-defining moment. We've all shared that moment, but 99% of the sheep are going to try and return to the way it was before. Those are the people who are going to be fighting for scraps in the future.

If you want to be the person who makes the mark and you want to be remembered in history, you need to change now. The world is only going to continue to change post this moment.

If you don't, maybe you'll have a year or five years, but you aren't going to survive any of the fucking shitstorm that's going to continue to come.

And what's going to come? You're only going to see governments continue to fuck up their currencies. You're only going to continue to see bitter conflicts as people start fighting for basic resources, food, shelter, and even water.

What you're further going to see is all of the ways that you thought you could do business, all of the ways you thought you could generate revenue and get your exit and get your legacy, are going to be gone.

Why are you even doing this, businessman? Are you just looking for an exit? Okay, if you're just looking for an exit, what the fuck are you going to do after that?

If you are trying to make a legacy play and trying to hand it down to the next generation, what are you going to have to give to them if your business dies in five years? You won't have anything.

You, as a business executive, need to grapple with the fact that humanity is hurtling towards destruction. You have an opportunity to be a part of the solution, to actually carve out a way that humanity could actually survive, because if climate change doesn't kill us, we're going to kill each other first.

Governments aren't going to solve this; they've proved incapable of solving this. But the things that can solve this are humans working together. Bridging that gap, getting a unique, core understanding that is bigger than any one individual state, any one individual community.

You need to start thinking about this and adopting it now because otherwise, you will be left in the dustbin of history. And if you're left in the dustbin of history, you are just going to be the same as everyone else who is either going to be obliterated in the next global pandemic that hits us, who're going to be ravaged by the next war the next time Putin decides to invade another country, or China, or any one of the nefarious actors that exist out there.

How will you be able to survive? Who's going to bail you out? Do you think your government's going to bail you out? The government won't do it. With what money?

This isn't even a slight at the business executive of yore. I've met many smart business executives, and regardless of their age, this is purely down to a mindset. It's hard, I get it.

When you go through something as traumatic as we have for the last two years, you might think, 'hey, that was so awful, I don't ever want to experience that again.' So you retreat to a place of safety, mental safety.

More often than not, that mental safety is going to be a place in the past. That's nostalgia. This is a common human tactic we try to apply whenever we're faced with anything truly life-threatening to ourselves. We go back to the times where we felt safe.

We can't look to the future to feel safe because it hasn't happened yet, so we have to go back to the past. We have to go back to our past, or a collective past, where we find those moments where we felt safe, nurtured, and comforted. It's like the simple concept that every human on the planet is just a child who's done varying rotations around the sun.

Because of this phenomenon, everyone's thinking about this in the same way. 'How can I get back to safety? How can I get back to a world that previously existed?'

Why are you racing back to those ways of doing things?

This is now directed to the business executive: Why have you gone your entire life challenging the 'sheeple,' for lack of a better term? You've gone your entire life thinking, 'hey, how can I create a business that succeeds?'

Most people don't even do that. Most people don't even think this way. This is a very overused idea. I know there's a lot of people who talk about entrepreneurship in terms of hustles, and "think differently," blah, blah, blah.

But the business executive? You've actually done it. So why, given that you've built an entire career on doing things differently from the rest of humanity, are you now trying to act exactly the same as everyone else?

– Patrick Ward, August 2023

Chapter 1

Source of the Problem

I'm a big believer in the fragility of civilization. We like to think that humans today are so advanced. We've done so many crazy and cool things, so many inventions, blah blah blah.

But if you actually look at it, it does not take a lot to completely wipe out what humanity has put together.

One only has to look at a couple of the natural disasters that have happened in the last 20 years, like Hurricane Sandy and Hurricane Katrina. Look at all the costs incurred for the cities affected.

Newsflash for CEOs: that's going to happen with increasing frequency.

You might reason, 'oh, well, I invest in green technology, I invest in sustainability, I don't need to worry about those things, the market dictates that we will solve that problem and I can continue running my business in exactly the same way as I always have.' To that, I would say that we do not even know the full ramifications of everything we are building.

For example, say we build something that yields carbon capture, and we're putting less carbon into the atmosphere. But we don't know its impact. It could imbalance the environment in some other unforeseen way.

If everything is changing, if all the variables keep shifting, if none of the expectations or institutions that you have built your entire business model on, and your entire brain on, exist, what can you trust?

You're reading this book because the only thing you can rely on is the one thing that has carried humans throughout history.

That's adaptability.

Humanity has been all about adaptability throughout its entire existence. We've adapted to climates, we've adapted to different ways of organizing ourselves, we've adapted to different forms of business.

You might say you're an adaptable person, but is your business adaptable? Your business needs to be resilient. It needs to be agile.

And you can't just pay it lip service. You can't just create a little innovation lab inside your company and put 1% on R&D, which is what most of the big guys do. They go, "there's 1% R&D. That's fine. That's enough to fix it."

No.

You need agility and resilience built in from the very start, throughout your entire organization.

There are two big components to what a CEO values.

There's the more functional component, which relates to CEOs and C-suite executives in general. They care about growing the companies they represent. Why is that? Because financial success, by most measures of humanity, is deemed as the ultimate success.

Now you'll find the contrarian folk who will go in other avenues, but generally, your C-suite executive is not a complete anarchist when it comes to that sort of thing. This is because they've come up, presumably, through various corporate tracks, and they're at least fairly conventional on that front.

But there's a bigger piece aside from success. That success could be a lifestyle company where the CEO is just trying to generate revenue over the course of their lifetime or trying to position it towards some form of acquisition, like IPO. You'll have some CEOs talk in those terms, saying they want to sell their company in five years, or hoping to exit for X million dollars.

You're not going to get those outcomes if you keep thinking in the ways of the past.

Then there is the legacy play. This doesn't necessarily speak to every C-suite executive, but at least in my experience, a fairly large portion are thinking about their legacy in some capacity.

That can mean everything from them being a magnanimous individual who thinks they are going to change the world (and more often than not, they're not, even if they're on the level of someone like Elon Musk), to them at least thinking about, 'what am I setting up for the future of either my name or my family?'

That also is worth taking into consideration, given the themes we are talking about in this book, because the CEO who's going to continue to operate on past business metrics is likely to be fundamentally whacked by what's going to happen.

You're likely going to have more pandemics. You're likely going to have more supply chain issues. You're likely going to have all the usual ways that you grow a business become much more challenging. Accessing credit from various financial intermediaries is going to get more expensive.

You're going to have to do more with less.

I think the path to getting the ultimate talent is going to be so critical because you're going to finally have a corporate structure, or a company structure, that has agility and resilience built into it from the very beginning, whereas the majority of company structures that exist to this day are easily wiped out by pandemic number two, easily wiped out by another war, or easily wiped out by friction in the oil supply.

Some C-suite executives and business owners just need a little bit of the fear of God put into them. I think they're still operating with the same mental models because maybe it's something they learned from an MBA once.

That's one side of the equation.

Then there was the hullabaloo about Chat GPT. I put this chapter's topic to the bot through a variety of different prompts, and the thing that made me angriest was how its answers involved something about outsourcing with cost.

I am tired of this. I thought, 'damn, this is exactly what I've always said that AI will never do.' AI is great at pattern recognition and spinning up things from the past, but it will never originate a unique idea.

At first, I was mad, but then, not surprised.

Because, of course, that's the mental schema that most of these C-suites have filtered down through their organizations, and that's how they are treating these types of concepts, like outsourcing, like distributed teams. They view it merely as a cost-play in terms of minimizing costs rather than a way to gain a sustainable competitive advantage for their businesses.

Every C-suite executive that I meet falls victim to something that the finance industry has known its entire life, which is that past performance is not indicative of future results. It's a little disclaimer that is put on every financial product.

Yet every CEO decides how to run their business based on financial models provided to them by accountants, which are archaic. They also decide how to run their business based on business strategies that have not been battle tested. They are usually coming from a variety of high-end MBAs that are just not that academically rigorous.

Why? Because most of business theory came out of the Industrial Revolution and then during the 1960s and the 1970s. It does not have a long tenure in terms of being repeatable for humans, nor does it have a high chance of repeatability.

It really gets infuriating because these fields act like there is one prescriptive notion for how to create a business. Yes, maybe your old model gave you access to capital. Maybe it allowed you to grow during the 1980s, the 1990s, and the 2000s. Maybe it allowed you to grow because a lack of regulation meant things were relatively easy.

But if you really think about the world of business, you need to tap into something far more expansive and far more uniquely human, rather than just relying on a couple of archaic models that haven't even really seen the true ravages of disruption.

Human history, by and large, has been dictated by wars, plagues, and conquests, yet we've had an era of unbridled prosperity since about the 1950s or 1960s. That is a blip in the evolution of human history.

Now if we're going to act like scientists, and I would encourage every C-suite executive who claims to love data (they all love to say they're data-driven), to actually look at it. If you look at the information over the course of human history, why would you think the last 50 years is more worth investigating than, realistically, the last 10,000 years of homosapiens' existence on this planet?

The funny thing is, the modern financial system that we operate under is a little bit older than those business strategies that I mentioned. You can trace it back to the 1600s.

This is imperative to understand, for all the CEOs who declare, "oh, I'm ready to change. I'm always adapting my business. I'm always looking at the next opportunity." To that, I would ask, "are you?" Because you're looking within the very narrow framework that exists right now.

You're looking through a lens, and you don't realize how many assumptions you're making.

You're making assumptions that inflation will continue to be handled. You're making assumptions that raw materials will continue to be in abundance or enough abundance for your venture. You're making assumptions that your target market will still have enough money to buy your damn products and services.

The problem is there's still too much belief in institutions, as well as these systems that have grown up around us.

Business theory is archaic.

Disruption is only going to keep happening. That's the natural disaster angle.

The third problem is the data. Business owners and executives keep looking at data to inform their decisions when the data has been skewed by the past.

The two areas that it traditionally takes to grow a business will also become problematic in the near future. I'm talking about line of credit and supplies.

Everyone just keeps saying that the supply chain will be solved, and that angers me. If you haven't got the fact that the supply chain is tenuous from the last two years, you're going to be really shocked at how much more that gets obliterated. Then there's line of credit. American businesses, since basically post-World War II, have been used to easy access to credit. That is unlikely to persist as well.

You might say that these are assumptions, I say the traditional ways you've been able to grow your business will evaporate.

Adaptability

Stop flexing about how you're so adaptable and BE adaptable.

Don't look at how you're better than a couple of competitors, even if you're top of your market.

You think the disruption that's going to happen is going to care about that? Of course not. It'll obliterate entire industries, entire cities, and entire countries.

You need to think in terms of how you can build adaptability as a practice. How can you build adaptability as an ethos? Even if you think you are the most adaptable person, are your customers adaptable? Are your employees adaptable? Is your inanimate business structure adaptable? And is it prepared to take on every disaster known?

That's what every business needs to be for the future. It can't just be about being able to survive a recession. It needs to be able to survive a recession, institutional fragmentation, supply chain obliteration, health crises, and wars all at once. If you've built a business that can do that, you've built a business that can do anything.

A failure to adapt would be pretty easy to explain because, and this is not even about ripping up capitalism, it often gets thrown in that category. If you're looking at the way capital has absorbed different functions over the course of its time, what has happened is that capital will get deployed, usually through financial intermediaries, and provide itself to businesses in order to stake a claim over a certain market.

This is the whole debt-fueled theory of finance, and it's made sense for a long time, and it made sense when there were still realms to conquer. When this modern monetary theory came about, it started in the era of colonialism be- cause there was still some world to expand into.

Then we started industrializing. We made improvements, used machines, we used automation, and so on. That's the next domain.

Now we're getting into another domain, and we're close to realizing this promise of the mind. If you look at the last ten years, where have all the big companies been residing? In software and in things that control a person's mind.

When you look at that, you realize we have an increasingly limited amount of domains to conquer. Because of that, you think that you are adapting to change. CEOs think they're adapting; they think they're looking at the world and how to respond to it.

But you're only responding to the world in terms of financial quarters. You're responding to the world in terms of what's the next crisis. You're not responding to the world in the overarching centuries-long themes that we've been building towards.

It doesn't matter if you adapt to December of this year. It doesn't matter if you adapt to Quarter 2 of next year. You're doing false, miniature adaptations rather than a whole-scale mind shift. This is what you need to be applying to your entire business.

I guess, to this point, it's not even about the failure to adapt; it is the illusion of adaptation. Because every CEO of every company that has ever failed has thought they were in the right. They thought, 'oh, I'm trusting the data. I'm running a business correctly.' Yes, there are a few who get in over their heads, but by and large, those are the exceptions.

Most CEOs do think they're being good stewards of their business until they're not. Until they're filing for bankruptcy, until the company gets bought out. This is more than a one-business problem. It's going to be a whole-scale and system-wide problem. That's why you can keep doing your little adaptations within the one to five years scale, maybe you might even last 10 years.

But you won't last longer with what's about to come.

The hellscape that could be ahead comes about because most businesses have been set up within incredibly similar environments. They have been set up regionally, domestically, and citywide without much thought.

What are you going to do when your city starts running out of water? What are you going to do when food prices start to skyrocket to the point that your consumers can't buy your products because they're just trying to feed themselves?

When everything that you've known about how your business can operate, from what you paid your suppliers to how much you can charge your end customers, collapses. When all of that gets thrown out, you, like your customers, are going to be fighting for the scraps.

You can't run a functional business in a world like that.

You might immediately say, "that's okay, I'm a multinational, I operate across all corners of the globe." That's not even the full answer either, because just saying "I'll be a multinational," means that you still need access to credit.

What are you going to do when central banks start running out of money? Look at how many countries are in debt. Huge debt. Very few countries are in surplus. What happens when that debt needs to be repaid? When the Piper needs to be paid?

What happens when all that free money from the financial institutions and banks that you've become accustomed to going to for a line of credit or other access to capital disappears? Do you have enough cash flow to deal with that reckoning? Probably not. You're going to have to pay your loan sharks or whoever holds your debt.

That's another disruption.

The other big horror is, back on the multinational point, suddenly, you are at risk of global conflicts and global supply chain issues that are only going to proliferate because we're running out of raw materials. They're all getting more expensive.

If there's one thing that should scare everyone, it's something very simple that's happening right now. It's chips. We can't even make enough microchips for the world's computer processing. At the same time that every 'futurist' is out there in the world, extolling the benefits of quantum computing, AI, and the cloud. It all needs chips to run. Where are the raw materials?

So much of the world is built on physical infrastructure. Physical infrastructure that's not just here in the States. We hear a lot of the time about infrastructure decaying here, but there's a lot of infrastructure that's decaying all over the world. It only takes a little bit of that to crumble.

As more and more of it disintegrates, it's going to take out communities, it's going to take out cities, and more importantly, for you business owner, it's going to take out your business without a moment's hesitation.

You don't have to just worry about the environmental issues. The problem with climate change is that it looks like such a huge issue, such a big thing to overcome, that we often just get scared of it.

We look at the environmental factors, and when our reality doesn't match that, we excuse it. "Oh, okay, we've had a few more natural disasters in the last couple of years, but you know, I'm sure it won't be too bad." But that's not the only problem.

The problem is that a catastrophic hellscape is about to happen because everything you know is going to go under at the same time. It's not just going to be environmental. All the social, financial, corporate structures and systems, and institutions that you have relied upon are going to be pushed to the brink.

And you might think, "well, they'll be resilient." But why? Why would any of them be resilient? They weren't built to be resilient. They weren't built for this level of testing. Realistically, most of the institutions that have been used to create our modern American capitalist system don't go further back than about the 1890s. They've never been battle tested. They've never had to deal with a truly astronomical issue.

Think about what happened two years ago. We had a

pandemic that was a flu. I'm not minimizing the deaths, but realistically, that pandemic was not even that horrendous. It was a flu that the majority of people survived. Yet it caused absolute untold havoc.

Shipping ports closed down. What did that mean? Suddenly, the few raw materials that still existed couldn't get to manufacturing and processing plants. Suddenly, you were getting less stuff being built. Now consumers are paying higher prices, now we've got inflation. Now businesses are worried about how they will retain their staff.

Now put all of that together and consider that it was only a taster. That was an appetizer for what's about to come.

You need to really consider how you can set up a business to face some of the most unprecedented horrors of the world.

Dante's Nine Circles of Hell don't even begin to describe what we will all face in our lifetime.

Business Theory

So, what can you, as a CEO or leader, do tomorrow?

A CEO can stop holding their business models to these restrictive accounting, double-entry-based theories that have persisted now for a number of years.

The CEO might be asking what they can do instead of that.

What they can do instead is get back to simplicity in their business model. What they really need to monitor is the money coming in and the money going out.

They need to look at those two areas within a couple of lenses. With the money coming in, they need to look at who's buying their product and why they are buying it. Is there any reason, in the next several years, that someone would not want to buy your product or service? Is there anything that could happen to that person that would cause them to stop buying your product or service?

Get away from the numbers and return to humanity.

What are the commonalities among your buyers? How important is your product or service to them? Is it just nice to have? Then you should be really worried. Is it imperative that your buyer has your product or service for them to live their day-to-day lives? Now you're probably onto something stronger.

You've got to look at the cost structures on the other side of the equation. What's going out?

This is where you shelve your ego.

Are there materials that you use for your business that are going to be in short supply? Time to start looking at the alternatives. Are there ways you can get recycled materials? Are there ways you can be more sustainable so that you minimize your business's dependency on future raw materials?

On the flip side, look at the employees. That's where you've got to be very rigorous. Don't think, 'which of my employees are doing critical work?' You want to think in terms of 'where is the best possible person for each of these functions? And regardless of where they live, could I attract them to work for my company?'

Because this is where business owners get egotistical. They start thinking in these terms of an onshore person being better than an offshore person. No, they're not. Maybe for some areas, but not for every area.

Have a really hard look at yourself and say, 'how can I be the most efficient in making sure that I have got the best possible talent, regardless of location? Have I got the best possible materials, and am I serving a need for customers that is an absolute necessity for them?'

If you throw those three things together, then you should have a model for how much you can realistically make. Not only is that good from a financial sense, but you've done one thing that others haven't, which is that you've accumulated the best talent.

You are going to need the best talent if we're going to solve these problems going forward so that they're ready, like you are now, to adapt and to embrace change.

Disruptions

You can't stop pandemics, wars and natural disasters. They will always happen.

Look at the distributed companies that exist today. There are a number of companies in my particular industry, for example, that have operations based in Ukraine. Those operations got pretty whacked in the last year, as you can imagine.

You can't stop that, but you can build resiliency. You build resiliency, funnily enough, in the same way you build a business resiliency plan.

Every Californian company has a resiliency plan for earthquakes. Why don't you expand that by starting a process for your business to move towards distributed teams?

It's not that you'll avoid these natural disasters, but you will create small pockets of yourself. You'll create pockets where your business can continue to operate, regardless of location. By not consolidating everyone in one headquarters or even one domestic market, you build in multiple points of failure rather than a single point.

That is imperative.

You actually get an additional benefit by doing this. For example, if we have a pocket in Argentina. Their economy is atrocious right now. The funny thing is, for our business model, that means we're now getting cost efficiencies for our payroll while still being the same.

That's what you get when you start building these multiple points of failure. What might seem like a disruption can actually get you an opportunity.

Those opportunities only come about if you're not dependent on one location, one city, even one country. You can start to diversify that risk as well as diversify the opportunity.

Data

The problem with most data is that you're constantly looking at statistics of past companies or competitors or other industry sources, all of which are based on previous frameworks of the past.

The only solution is increasing your proficiency in forecasting (though that's difficult to do). If you aren't forecasting appropriately now, you need to get on and do it. And if you are, you need to become a statistician. You need to start looking at the data every time you forecast your results. How closely aligned are your expectations to the statistics?

You might say, "oh, well, I already do forecasting. I'm already looking at my inputs and my outputs." Okay. Did you predict the pandemic? No? No one could have predicted it. Perhaps not. But did you even try?

You need to start building the models to not just look at the past way of doing business, but to also incorporate future threats.

You can do it. You can give them a weighting.

If you're telling me that's too hard, I say, "well, when you look at your pipeline of deals, you give them a weighting based on what you expect to close or not close. Why couldn't you do the same thing with natural disasters?"

Why couldn't you look at how many experts predict a pandemic in the next five years and put a 30% weighting on a pandemic happening?

You won't need to have the tough conversations if you get really good at forecasting. 'Do I have to rip up my business? Do I have to sell it for scrap? Do I have to go bankrupt?' You won't have to do all the things that you don't want to do because the pride of most business owners is to be able to grow a business that survives shocks to the system.

There are many who have gone through the Arab oil crisis of the 1970s. They went through the boom and bust of Dot-Com. They went through the GFC.

I commend those companies because of that, but get ready for a whole lot more disruption.

Assumptions

The only thing that you can rely on is your business

fundamentals; looking after your people and looking after your customers.

That's not to say you can't find good and innovative ways of partnering with suppliers. That's not to say you can't find interesting ways to access credit. But you can't realistically rely on those systems persisting.

We don't know when these catastrophic events will happen, but we do know they'll happen in a variety of sequences. You will want to have built your business in a way that ensures that you have the internal ability to stay afloat, regardless of any outside forces that happen. Even if the institutions that you've relied upon want to help you, they won't even be able to. They won't have the resources they need.

If you think you're ill-prepared reading this so far, I can tell you the institutions that have dotted this country's history are even less prepared than you.

They'll be the first to crumble, but you can rise from the ashes.

If you've read all this so far, you've probably felt, 'well, shit, this is really bleak. This is really depressing. What should I do? Why should I do anything?'

Well, you must do something, because this is actually the most enormous opportunity for every business owner.

It isn't going to be governments. And it isn't going to be an individual person.

We are going to rely on an enormous number of people coming together to literally save humanity.

You've told me you want your legacy. More often than not, the business owner has relied on their legacy to be just about business, but wouldn't it be incredible if your legacy was contributing to the saving of humanity? That is a legacy that will stand the test of time far more than any individual business.

Look back to Rockefeller. He was the richest man in the world during the 1930s. You ask a handful of people outside of economists or history teachers, and most people have forgotten him. If they do remember him, it's, "oh, I think there's a plaza in New York City named after him."

That man is in living memory. There are still people alive on this earth today that were around when he was, and he's been forgotten.

But you look at the people who last through history. They're people like Jesus, Gandhi, and Mother Teresa, people who do enormous things for humanity.

As a business owner, you have an opportunity to be one of those people.

Chapter 2

Searching Talent

In today's world, where disruption is the new norm, building a business that will be resilient and achieve long-term success is a challenge.

Many businesses limit themselves by viewing outsourcing as a problem. There is a pervasive misconception that outsourcing is a substandard option which further exacerbates the problem of companies settling for mediocrity when there is a whole world of talent out there waiting to be tapped.

For centuries, human civilization has been primarily characterized by hyper-localized communities where people would live and work within the same area for their entire lives. It is only in the past few hundred years, with the advent of technology like trains, planes, and other transportation, that we began to connect with and do commerce in areas right across the planet.

If we take a close look at the various industries that originated in the Industrial Age and earlier, we can see the influence of local communities in their development. Fast forward to the Information Age, and we suddenly find ourselves with unprecedented levels of real-time communication that allow us to connect with people all over the world.

The first concept of outsourcing came into existence in the 1980s. We turned that early model to India and began with simple functions, like customer support and call centers, which gradually grew into more complex, mission-critical functions. This era of expansion was the heyday of outsourcing, where we had a front office staff that was "domestically based" in the Western world, and a back office staff in India or The Philippines.

All these outsourcing regions had two things in common. They were places where spoken English was reasonably widespread and labor cost little. As companies expanded to these regions, outsourcing gained its reputation as a low-cost and economical option for businesses.

Customers weren't thrilled because culture clashes began to arise, and they perceived that they were getting substandard service from outsourced staff. This perception was inaccurate because difficulties that arose were a result of companies' failures to correctly implement their outsourcing. The model, in and of itself, was accurate.

During the 2000s, and especially around the 2010s era, when it was no longer a new concept, people started talking about different ways to solve this problem.

Over the last 20 years, people began to talk about solving the 'problem' of outsourcing. This talk became particularly prevalent in the last ten years as the concept has grown older.

Some would argue that India is half a day out, and because you're not speaking to outsourced staff at the same time, projects are delayed or disrupted and that means you're not delivering your best quality service.

Others would talk about cultural clashes and argue that companies needed to outsource in regions of the world similar to their region of origin. For instance, they would argue that American-based businesses should seek outsourcing opportunities in nations that have a strong shared history with the US.

Then there are others who would talk about business expectations if a company were to outsource in a country where people work to live versus countries where people live to work.

Amidst all these arguments, we miss out on asking the fundamental question of whether or not outsourcing is really a problem in the first place. There is an underlying assumption that outsourcing is substandard and, therefore, inferior to domestic-based production. There is a belief that it needs to be addressed so we can finally realize the promise of the gains of cost. This is, fundamentally, the crux of why I hate how this entire industry has been conceptualized, and I always go back to one of the following key examples.

In the world of software development, the average software developer that comes out of a US-based coding camp has done 16 weeks of training. They've learned the basics of C++ and maybe a little bit of the history of computer programming. They are not battle ready at all at this point. Yet, they get to call themselves a software developer and get to charge six figures for initial employment.

Compare that to an Argentinean developer who has done five years of training, which is basically a master's-level equivalent of education in the US. They have usually worked alongside other developers inside a firm or company for several years. Only after their extensive training do they get to call themselves a developer, and they are charging $20,000 a year in wages, if not less. Even if we remove the cost from that equation, objectively speaking, that developer is a better developer than the one trained in America. Why is this the case? Well, one institutional factor is that the government in Argentina supports a very young childhood education model for STEM education.

Regardless of what particular fields you need to hire in,

you should not be limiting your business to the talent pool that exists in your local region. Instead, you need to look at where the masters are in each of the fields your business requires. By building a business where you hire the best staff for each function, you can create a more resilient business compared to one that has many areas vulnerable to disruption.

In the previous chapters, we talked about how many disruptions are coming down the pipeline. Having the best talent in your business means having the best minds that can help you adapt and innovate. Hiring the best staff for each function ensures each aspect of your business is optimized for success, making it less susceptible to potential disruptions. Being a business owner doesn't mean you know everything, so having the most talented staff at hand can be one of the most effective ways to adapt to inevitable disruptions.

If you knew everything about your business, you wouldn't hire a single person because you would be able to do it all yourself, or you'd be able to teach robots to do it. The very fact that you engage the employment of any other single individual is because they know something about their specific domain of expertise that you don't. Following this line of thinking, why would you sell yourself short and choose the "C" player just because they live in your region or your city? Why would you not get the "A" player regardless of their location?

Why do you have your sales and marketing staff primarily based in the US? Because you're going to be having them speak to customers, and having that level of cultural familiarity and cultural nuance is often really important.

Why are you going to have your design staff based in Romania or South America? Because the best design agencies come from those regions.

Why are you going to find Eastern European talent to augment your near-shore or onshore developers? Because they are the best bang for your buck you're going to get there.

I use these examples to articulate a stronger system and vision for how you should conceptualize your business. You piece together A-grade talents, and make a system of communication to fit around them rather than building a business to fit your needs and then trying to fit people into it. I'm advocating for a talent-first approach and a talent-first system to build a business.

It is self-centered to build a business based on what you want to accomplish first and geared towards your own needs, rather than the actual business's needs. In order for your business to survive every shock that this world is going to throw at it, you must first know the core components of the business that allow it to survive.

Firstly, does your business have a sustainable competitive advantage? This is based on the standard business theory of whether the business does something that no one else does. But as we have witnessed in the past several decades, this doesn't even matter right now because, in a year or two, another business might come along and have the exact same thing you have. So that's out of the window.

Second, you might think you can compete on price, and you're the Walmart of your industry, selling the cheapest things possible. It only takes someone else to come up with a slightly better way of doing it, and then your advantage is gone.

Your business might take a different approach and offer a premium service. Maybe you are the absolute "white glove" experience, and you cater to the highest of high net-worth individuals. But, you already know that they are some of the most fickle people in the world and can be quite unpredictable.

So, if these are all the standard ways that people approach business to achieve success, it is worth questioning if any of them are going to work.

We can refer to this idea around the concept of Moore's Law which states that technology either doubles in speed or halves in size every 18 months. This leads to a rapid increase in the rate of change that happens in our world, which means that the one area that your business can rely on to constantly power you into the future is its talent. If your talent is always on the bleeding edge of what's possible, you can be assured they will have the finest ideas to tackle whatever challenges are thrown at your business. Having that talent is a key advantage that could see your business thrive for the next ten, twenty, fifty, or even a hundred years. If you get the talent part of your business right, then everything else falls into place.

There are three main factors to consider when sourcing talent: communication, technology, and a mindset shift. While communication and technology facilitate the sourcing process, the mindset shift is a change in approach or strategy for actually identifying and attracting top talent.

This is not only about accepting that people from different regions of the world can be part of your business. It's also about recognizing that you will need to adapt your company's operations based on people's cultural expectations. This is absent from American-based businesses' strategies all the time. They launch a business in a country outside the US without bothering to get a full understanding of its cultural nuances, and the business fails as a result.

If you cultivate an "appreciation" of different cultures, your business will actually improve as a result. You will have a true diversity of thought in your organization that catches any blind spots, any cognitive biases, and any cultural biases which ultimately makes your business more resilient.

Cost is still an important consideration.

And when you hire the best staff from around the world, you

are still going to accrue a cost advantage, and ironically it's not just about paying less. In many cases, the lower cost is due to exchange rates rather than "underpayment."

For example, I pay my virtual assistants $1,200 a month. To an American company, $1,200 a month is a small amount, it's peanuts. Yet to the Indian virtual assistant, that's about double the market rate, and it allows him to put his wife through private hospital healthcare so she can deliver their baby with peace of mind.

You can think about your business's approach to costs as something that is more than just efficient spending. It could be something that is actually improving living standards and saving business capital. There will be significantly more costs for the business owner who still believes they need to hire a person in Los Angeles or San Francisco. That hire is going to cost two times, three times, or even four times as much as a similarly talented person in South America.

Transforming Communication

Communication styles have very much been oriented towards in-person and in-office interaction since corporations have existed. This is not to say there aren't good components of in-person work, but why is it the most inefficient?

It comes back to Henry Ford and his Model T era. At the time, the eight-hour workday made sense because it was a significant downgrade from the 12 to 16-hour workday that was common beforehand. It continued post-World War II, into the 1950s to the 1980s, when most people were going into offices, working in cubicles, and the only way that they communicated with one another was by stopping at each others' desks or sitting in conference rooms and meetings that were, by and large, pointless.

This methodology went unquestioned for decades because it was the only way to communicate effectively. Even if you were communicating from the West Coast of America to the East Coast, you were using spotty conference lines, and maybe you missed a lot of what the other person was saying. Long-distance communication was hindered by poor conference lines and wasn't really suitable for any form of real-time communication. Because of that, business operations stayed primarily localized.

The problem with this method of communication is that it is oriented towards a very specific style of communication that works for more extroverted people. As more data is gathered, several statistics that still persist to this day report that the average American office worker does 56% of real work in an eight-hour day. That is an appalling figure and barely meets a passing grade.

This sort of communication style is bound to fail because it was set up to support a generic, amorphous person. It has never been perfect for getting the work done. We still see this style implemented, even as companies have wrestled their workers back into the office. It's quite funny because this phenomenon of interrupting someone at their desk, has been brought into the spotlight once again, and people have gone, "Hey, wait a minute, that's actually a really non-constructive way of getting work done." It interrupts people when they're getting into a flow state and trying to tackle big ginormous tasks.

The solution is to look at the communication options available to you right now. To build communication styles appropriate for the person, rather than feeding the ego of the business owner, who may be getting a buzz from people surrounding them regardless of output or productivity.

Asynchronous communication is one communication style that is available to us right now, thanks to technological advancements. You can use Slack for instant communication and communicate your project briefs using Loom videos. You can schedule meetings only when they're relevant, and you can do that in different time zones based on when different teams are awake or asleep. You're able to assign them tasks through project management dashboards. As an individual worker, you can even block off time for deep-focus work.

In recent years, there has been a greater appreciation for this approach as people realize they don't need to do ten menial tasks that only serve to make them look busy, as opposed to three solid and noteworthy tasks they could have accomplished if they were following their own work rhythm and weren't constantly interrupted.

So what's the prescription here for the business owner? It's about understanding the goals that each function of your business is trying to accomplish and gearing them up to be able to communicate in a way that works for them.

If you have a software development team working on building your product, you can leave it to their project manager to have a weekly stand-up with them. They'll have their tasks and backlogs to work on as they move through the week, and you can make them responsible for updating a progress system asynchronously. It allows you to observe the work that's been done, rather than them having to tell you in seven or eight different meetings that interrupt the flow of their work.

Similarly, you do not need your sales team on a sales floor. You can record their calls with something like Gong, and you will be able to listen in. You can have their managers and coaches listen in on those calls and hear how they're doing so you can provide the necessary training and mentorship needed.

Looking through every single department of your business, you will find a lot of pointless, redundant communication and meetings. That meeting could have been an email, and that email could have been a Slack message, and that Slack message might not have needed to be sent at all.

It is tempting to believe that the reduction of frequent communication might result in a less tightly-knit company. However, the opposite is true. By reducing this burden, you will get people who are actually driving the business forward and creating impact, versus doing busy work.

Workers get disengaged from their work when they feel like what they do doesn't matter. Unfortunately, that is how the cadence of corporate communication, up until this point, has left employees feeling. It has created a culture where playing office politics takes precedence over the productive work that employees care about, the work that you should care about as a business owner.

Maximizing Human Potential

Technology, especially the tech we have today, excels at automating the grunt work, the menial tasks, and essen-tially all the back-office work systems of an employee. In the same way that you split your business into the front office and back office, so too does an individual with their tasks.

The front office tasks of an individual are the big areas of impact, the things they care about and feel passionate about. A quick example would be salespeople who are spending their time talking with customers, delivering proposals, and understanding why people are buying. Their front office tasks are all about messaging those prospects in a way that gets them to engage with your business.

The back office tasks, on the other hand, are things like updating the CRM and most people hate doing that, which makes sense because these are machine-like tasks that are ideal for automation. This is where you need to be thinking about applying technology.

The technology that you use for your tech stack, tied to both business operations and communication, needs to be viewed as something that can benefit your workers. You need to think, 'How can I help my staff be more human every day? How can I remove more of the coin-operated-machine tasks that they have to do?'

At the end of the day, machines will always do what is oriented toward machines better than humans, and humans will always do what is oriented toward humans better than machines. As a business owner, you are in a perfect position right now, because machines are now intelligent enough to do certain tasks that humans once had to do. And therefore, you can begin to move your human workers away from machine-oriented tasks.

I've seen so many CEOs get frustrated with their sales team for not updating their CRMs perfectly, like not filling out all the fields. But why are they pushing a human to do what a machine could do better? As a business owner, wouldn't you rather your salespeople spend 100% of their time selling rather than 50% of their time updating a CRM? This is a prime example of how your technology stack can actually support human labor and be a great advantage. So make sure you invest in the right stack for your various employees.

On the other hand, you should not use technology as a crutch. You have to map out exactly what the technology needs of your employees are because all too often, software is oversold as something that will solve all of your business's problems. In reality, if you haven't solved the organizational problem first, nine times out of ten, the software will just amplify the problem that already exists in your business.

Done the right way, the use of technology can support many human endeavors that can unlock an entirely new level of productivity from your talent. By hiring based on potential and leveraging a technology that works cohesively and symbiotically with your team, you activate their potential to achieve even greater levels of success.

Shift Towards Focusing on Talent

The world we live in has woken up to a two-way street of working, which is the main reason we need to focus on talent. When you started your business, you may have been used to the corporate hierarchy. Now, the corporate hierarchy still exists, but the power balance is no longer the same.

The employer used to have all the power because there were only a handful of companies in any given town or city for workers to access. But now we're competing on a global playing field; suddenly, workers have options. And if they have options, the only way you can compete is by demonstrating to them that you are not just like every other business. You need to be a business that operates in a manner that serves your workers.

For the longest time, CEOs and C-suite executives have talked about their talent without actually using that word to describe them. Instead, they refer to them as 'resources.' That is the most dehumanizing word imaginable to describe talent. It is almost akin to seeing a business's talent as mere cogs in a machine that spits out revenue. The fact that we are now talking about our workers as talent shows the powerful shift that has taken place in recent years.

Workers will fuel your business's success or failure. So, you need to shift your mindset to understand that your talent no longer serves you; you serve them. And by serving them correctly, they will achieve the results that you want for your business.

So how do you do that? You need to think very critically

about how effective your business structure is at helping your talent achieve success. You need to make sure that no matter what happens in a person's life, or career, they have achieved it because of your company, not in spite of it.

No company is going to look the same as it does today one year from now, so it might seem counterintuitive to focus on a business structure that is likely to change. But it's critically important to consider how you can support your talent today because it's your talent that will help your business get through tomorrow.

I will give you the following three lenses through which you can look at how you can support your talent: What are you doing to support them financially? What are you doing to support them professionally? What are you doing to support them personally?

If you support your talent in these three categories, you will unlock the biggest advocates for your business. They are going to spread the good word about your business, even after they leave. They are going to be far more fulfilled and engaged than your average worker, which means they are more likely to bring new ideas, new innovation, and new creativity to your business. Those engaged employees will directly benefit your business and not someone else's.

The average worker does 51% of the work. They do just enough not to get fired. But if you orient your business around them, you can unlock much more potential – 80%, 90%, 100%, or even 110%. Think of that differential. Think of all that extra industry, all that extra brain power, and all of that extra creativity that your business will be able to harness. Your business will benefit hugely if you can orient it around the needs of your talent rather than around your own desires.

In the past, businesses have taken it for granted that people will come to work for them. But things have changed. Nowadays, they will work for you if you give them a reason to, but if you don't, they will work against you.

Beyond Cultural Echo Chambers

For a long time, companies have focused on creating a culture similar to the culture of their leadership and customer base. This is one of the biggest fallacies we have today. Too many CEOs think that the entire world operates based on how they conceptualize it.

Naturally, what happens then is that organizations become echo chambers, leading to a lack of diversity in creation. Every organization is astutely aware that they do not want to create an echo chamber, and this is why you see terms like diversity, equity, and inclusion come about. However, companies are still viewing this through a very small lens, perhaps within racial or gender lenses, which limits their scope of insight. But when you're competing on a global scale, you have to think about diversity on a global scale.

In order to survive the next wave of innovation or crisis that will inevitably happen and impact your business, you need to anticipate it, have foresight, and map out an idea of what that future might be. If you can do this, you can build a future-oriented business that will be a forerunner in your industry. And the only way you can do this is by having people in your team who have their fingers on the pulse when it comes to different ways of working. This is the main reason why you need to stop orienting your business towards one particular market or mindset. You cannot limit your business to one nation when the security of your future hinges on succeeding on a global scale.

As a business owner, you need to think about your attributes, your background, your wealth status, your race, your sexuality, and your gender. Think of the advantages you could gain by embracing people from different backgrounds right across the world, and tapping into a knowledge base that is not limited to a Western or white male perspective.

Your business can benefit from expertise in various domains if it is exposed to multiple new ways of thinking. With multiple perspectives, you're suddenly able to anticipate changes, explore new supply chain models, engage with customers in ways that you could learn from, and tap into new customer bases. This type of globalized thinking is crucial for success compared to a localized approach that limits you where it doesn't need to.

Most manufacturing companies for the last 20 years have looked at China as the factory of the world. However, today, there are rising countries like Vietnam, Thailand, Malaysia, India, and Bangladesh. As a business owner, you might have thought there were only one or two regions where you could outsource production. But if you went and broadened the cultural perspective of your business, you could see these options before they became media headlines and position your business to be at the forefront of change.

We all know that most business advantages are accrued from change or disruption. The first 10% of businesses that adapt to change earn 90% of the resulting benefits. After that, every other organization is just fighting for scraps and all the initial advantages are gone. Early adaptation builds resilience into your business and that's why it is crucial to recognize that your personal or cultural perspective is only one of many, many more.

Maximizing ROI in Outsourcing

The focus of the initial points I discussed was on how to orient your business towards achieving big-picture goals by supporting and realizing the potential of your talents and changing the world.

However, as a business owner, you are naturally always thinking about the cost, which is maybe why you even picked up a book about outsourcing. Cost is always the number one thing. This is not a slight on you. Business owners inherently think about costs and what they are spending all the time. But viewing outsourcing solely on a cost-basis is short-sighted. Instead, consider the ROI.

As humans, we're wired to be more affected by the cost of something than the potential gain we might have missed out on. Because it's much harder for a human to concep-tualize something that they didn't have than it is to realize something that got taken away from them. That's why cost hurts you so much.

Thinking of outsourcing solely in terms of costs is short-sighted. You need to view it through the lens of ROI. What do I mean by that? Not only are you going to get the result from the different functions of your outsourced business for a lower cost, but you're also going to get a better result.

Instead of just focusing on the cost savings that come with outsourcing, reframe your thinking to consider the potential for a better result at a lower cost. Rather than thinking about the cheap cost of outsourcing, consider the marginal improvement you can gain by accessing better offshore talent compared to sticking with C-levels working in your local area.

You can do this in a variety of ways because outsourcing should not just be synonymous with "out of the country." Maybe instead of hiring from your local major city area, maybe you could hire from a rural area. That's also outsourcing. You might not think of it as outsourcing, Mr. CEO, but it is outsourcing.

Don't frame it in terms of 'I can't afford the best possible talent in my city.' Change your definition of 'best possible talent,' because it probably isn't in your city. Look at the global talent pool. Look at the function first, then see where the best talent of that function resides, and then go and get them by whatever means necessary. When you get that A-class talent, regardless of its location, you begin to get those incremental gains.

As you know, incremental gains equal compound results, which is why they are considered the eighth wonder of the world. Imagine what your business would look like if every single function and every single department was 10% better. The compounding effect of these improvements would result in a significantly better business.

I would love it if the whole world embraced this way of thinking, but I know the whole world won't because we as humans are tribal creatures. We like to stick with the pack, with what is the same. While that way of thinking has its own merits in appropriate situations, as a business owner thinking of outsourcing, this is where the opportunity to be a trailblazer lies. You are truly trying to create something that has never been created before.

Right now, we live in a world where multinational corporations try to take their way of thinking and plant it in a bunch of different regions to varying degrees of success. They'll do a fairly superficial layer of localization and see whether that works. Sometimes it does, sometimes it doesn't, but it's still within a very single vein. You can always tell an American company, an Asian company, and a European company.

With the level of interconnectedness we have today, you have the ability to create a truly global company and see success way beyond what you think is possible.

If another war breaks out or one market experiences a recession, it won't hold much significance to you, because you will have contingency teams in other regions. It doesn't matter if one government drastically increases compliance or wage rates because you've built the cost structure of your entire business to be flexible with that in mind.

The entire business that I am advocating for you to create is a business that is built on a level of margin, resiliency, and, ultimately, successful upside. Because you are going to have the best minds working for you. You are going to have access to the best forms of innovation, and you are going to be able to see opportunities arise before anyone else does. You are going to create the first global living organism of a business. A business that operates not in opposition to the world, but in conjunction with it.

It might seem aspirational and in defiance of conventional wisdom, so it requires significant courage, hard work, and determination to build your organization this way. Orienting your company around your talent, while undeniably becoming more and more relevant, can be a fickle endeavor. It is complicated by human factors. Your hard work might not pay off every time but you need to do this because the past is gone.

Corporations that dominated the world and subjugated humanity to their whims are now obsolete. If you truly care about the longevity of our society, and you feel inspired by this call-to-action I've prescribed to you, it will be easier for you to relish in the work that needs to be done because you understand that taking any other option will result in your business being swept aside by crises and inevitable tides of change.

Keeping your business operating in only one region of the world risks your talent leaving you and having the next supply chain crisis upend your entire business model. You've already seen it happen. One only has to look at the travel industry in 2020 to see how many businesses went under due to the Covid-19 pandemic.

This is a leap of faith. Most people are going to try and jump the chasm of this canyon, and most of them are going to get scared, look down, and plummet. You need to jump and go all the way, grab hold of the ledge on the other side, and pull yourself up.

It's not to say that taking a leap of faith won't be incredibly terrifying, but what's your alternative?

Chapter 3

Insourcing

With the aid of the internet and global talent, it is possible for a single business owner to run essentially every aspect of an outsourced business operation. However, most companies don't do this because it is impossible to create a tangible quality. It creates a business of cogs rather than a business that has what the industry likes to call "enterprise value".

As discussed in the previous chapter, I think the reason why we are trying to push people away from outsourcing is that it is solely viewed as a cost-saving measure. What I am advocating for, however, is a combination of insourcing and outsourcing as a strategy.

The goal is to underscore the idea that avoiding the crises of the future is not just about saving costs but about the flexibility of your business model. It's about your flexibility as an individual and the structure of how your business runs and makes money.

Realistically, taking a single approach to achieving a goal is impractical, especially with a future that is unpredictable. Full outsourcing as your only play creates a single point of failure. That only happens because you don't have the ability to shift your organization to respond to different threats. I have laid this one out, and this is fairly evident. We are aware that these threats are coming, but we don't know exactly which threat will happen at which time. No one can.

The reason why you will want to start thinking about insourcing, as a combination with outsourcing, is that insourcing starts to get to the heart of why you even run a business the way that you do.

You can run a fully outsourced business right now as a single person. You can outsource almost every single function with the advent of the internet and access to global talent.

But if you look at the biggest brand names and the most successful companies that have longevity, they're not like this at all. In a fully outsourced model, with only one person at the helm, where people are treated as mere cogs and mere functions, it becomes easier for disruption to occur. The person at the top is more likely to prioritize their individual goals because people aren't buying into something longer than a handful of years.

On the contrary, when employees are treated as valuable members and given a sense of ownership in the company's mission and vision, they are more willing to stay for an extended period of time. Unlike the former, it is not only geared towards the exit but rather towards a legacy. If you have read this far, it's fair to assume you found something compelling in this idea that I am proposing–to create a business model that will have a meaningful change and impact in the world of new commerce.

To put this simply, if you want a business that will last decades, you cannot have a fully outsourced company.

Let's look at insourcing and why its combination with outsourcing strategy is essential. There are certain functions of your business that are so intrinsic to its value that you need people, beyond yourself, who are going to dedicate full-time to your business with their mental capacity, their passion and their ability to come up with solutions.

Insourcing allows people to have a dedicated long-term mindset to solve problems that align with the company's vision, mission and values. These three concepts, which I'm sure most business owners are fairly familiar with, is what it all comes back to.

Why do they matter? Because this triad of concepts are fairly inherent in the human quest for meaning. In the last several decades in the Western world, many of the traditional meaning structures have decayed, some more than others. While the United States has preserved its religiosity fairly well compared to other Western nations, there has been a steep decline. But that doesn't mean that people are no longer craving meaning, and this is where you can provide a catalyst for them.

But if you're viewing your business with a short-term mindset and gearing your company towards exit, you will have people that buy-in financially instead of people that buy-in mentally, emotionally, and even spiritually.

These are the questions I want to pose to you right now, Mr. Business Owner: What about your company needs; someone who is completely dedicated in the same way that you are? What is the vision you are putting forward?

Let's say you're buying into the vision that I am laying out here in this book. You are also tired of how business has been exploitative, destructive and extractive of the world at large. Maybe you too believe there is a better way, one that can actually contribute to our society moving past these crises, one that actually improves the situation and the planet for the generations to come.

Start to articulate that and apply those ideas in your business. Which of the functions within your business relate most strongly to the realization of that vision? Whatever those functions are, that's where you want to be insourcing.

What do I mean by insourcing?

I don't necessarily mean that the person or that function needs to be exactly in the same location as you, but you need to realize there is always a significant shift between someone who is dedicated and incentivized based on long-term contracts versus those that are project-based and outsourced.

This is self-evident even in the ways that we historically pay people. When you pay someone in a contract capacity, you pay them for a fixed output, for a fixed project, or for a fixed amount of hours. It's clear when the contract ends. Maybe it renews, but there is a finality to it. When you bring someone in full-time, offer them stock and long-term incentives and keep your end of the bargain, suddenly you gain substantial employee capital, ingenuity, innovation and creativity all applied towards the larger picture and you ensure that your business, not only survives the next 5, 10, 20 years, but also thrives.

Think very critically about what those types of functions need to be, then think about how to articulate that vision, mission and values to attract the right type of person.

I mentioned religiosity earlier, and here's why you almost need to look there first rather than at other businesses. Other corporations, especially right now, struggle to inspire people to buy into a vision, but different religions excel at it. Pay attention to their language and how they empower their followers.

Look outside of the current reality of the business world; maybe look at charities and non-profit organizations. Don't easily dismiss their structure because, as a trailblazer and a pioneer, you need to have a comprehensive understanding of the dynamics of different organizations before you can create something truly innovative. You cannot copy the strategies, tactics and mindsets of the past and current corporations because they don't have the answer.

So that's my little piece of advice to you right now. Pay attention to the successful institutions where people are finding meaning. And as long as your intentions and integrity are pure, you too can be part of that new world where business equally contributes to people's life meaning and life purpose.

When you're bringing functions in-house with insourcing, you need to think about which areas of your business cannot fail in the future. This comes back to our earlier idea of "What do you see as the overarching theme of your company—a sustainable, competitive advantage if you will, that will endure and last the decades?"

It's not because your company won't change; every company does. Consider some of the biggest ones, like General Electric, as a classic example. They started building actual appliances. Now they are more like a financial company.

So, what are the common threads among businesses that have undergone morphing? When you look at those companies, you will start to uncover what areas need to be completely tied to you.

For example, if you are selling a technical product, you might think your engineering function is the most important to be in-sourced because your product is everything. And therefore, getting people who buy into the vision of what that product can achieve for the world is the most critical thing.

By contrast, if you are a service-oriented business, the most critical aspect is your people that serve your clients. Whatever that function is, once you've identified it, you need to go deep into what people care about.

There are three layers as to why people will choose a company to work for. The first is financial. You have to offer them a salary that is commensurate with their level of expertise. Always hire the A-players regardless of cost because they will always outperform B or C-players exponentially in terms of ROI. Don't skimp on talent.

The next step after you've hit them on that first financial bar is tying them to the long-term vision. Whether you want to do it in stock options or an incentive plan, that doesn't really matter because while tying their activities to the long-term vision is important, it is not enough for them to fully commit. This makes the next level of action essential to secure their complete buy-in.

Focus on professional development. Are your people going to continue to develop new skills? Are they going to continue to realize their professional potential? We're getting a little deeper here now. Have you laid out a career path for them? A particular vision? Laying out a vision for each of your employees that you have suitably in-sourced is really important. You need to map out not only what your journey is, and what your company aims to do over the decades, but, more importantly, what they can do over the course of their lifetime. We are now starting to get a little bit more into their mind. But that's still not enough.

We finally go to the lowest and deepest of levels. This comes back to the individual's self-concept, which is personal. What does a person really care about? This is where you have to be ruthless in finding people who are not just going to be attracted by the first two. Financial incentives and professional development are both great. You'll get great candidates for sure, but you'll only get candidates who see your company as a stepping stone to their next journey. And why wouldn't they? Most companies have only paid lip service and ignored the way that they call everyone "our family" without meaning it. This has been

Patrick Ward - Source

a systemic trend since about the 1980s when Reagan went fully into a neoliberal model, and correspondingly, the economists of the day also adhered to this mentality of prioritizing shareholder value above all else. Modern corporate culture has failed to demonstrate it cares about employees in the long term.

But people have become smarter and figured this out. They now think that if a corporation is not going to care about them in the holistic sense of their own being, they will evaluate employers based on the first two criteria. The financial criteria will be first, because that's always the most important to the vast majority of people, and then they will evaluate a business on professional development.

If you want to run counter to this and crack the code of what really matters to a person, such as why are they do-ing what they do? How do they want to be remembered? How do they want to talk about what they do to their kids? Once you speak about these intrinsic personal motivations down to a spiritual concept of how a person sees them-selves, you will be keeping those in-sourced employees and retaining them for the long term instead of just a year to do a function.

Here's the point. If you only speak to the first two layers, you are only going to end up getting an employee that is acting exactly the same as an outsourced resource. Sure, their 'contract' is longer than a handful of months, but you will still only have them for the specific time that they do a function, and then they leave to pursue their individual goals because their integration is not complete. That's not accruing their benefit.

What you want is someone who understands that third layer, the layer that you should have articulated to them to the point of obsession. We often think about obsession being not the most desirable trait. But in this case, it is. Because to truly change the world and to do it over a decades-long process, hiring cannot just be about money and professional development. You need people who are going to be as obsessed as you; they need to be personally invested. They need to be as invested as you. And you need to show that.

But as we all know, people have been betrayed here. People have been told to "follow your passion," and "do what you want to do." It is no surprise that companies have taken advantage of that by using all that language. As a result, you're going to have to go even harder here to show that, "hey, I'm not just saying that I care about your personal legacy as a hiring tactic. I care about it because I want you to join me for this decades-long transformation."

The first step to take is to identify the functions that you need in your business for decades to come. The next step is to make sure that you have a vision, mission, and values that speak to attracting the type of employee that will help you realize those functions that you need to have in-sourced for decades to come. You need to identify that 'A-class talent' and make sure they are compelled to join your venture.

From there, you need a measurement plan and strategy for how you keep those individuals because these in-sourced individuals are your key to whether you win or not. You need a rigorous plan that is agnostic of what they are doing today. This might seem counterintuitive, but because their role is inevitably going to change as part of their professional development, you are not going to be measuring them in the same way you should measure an outsourced function. Ultimately what you are trying to measure them on is more on the side of human capabilities rather than project-based capabilities.

Can they adapt to change? Can they be creative? How are they on critical thinking? Are they resilient? Do they show grit? These sorts of dimensions should be measured.

Finally, you need to think about how you are setting each of your insourced people up to succeed, so that if they succeed, your company succeeds, and therefore you realize your vision.

Identify Functions

When you're thinking about identifying the functions for insourcing, you're asking yourself one question: "what is the one thing that I hope my business will do better than any other business in the world?" It doesn't have to do that better than anyone else right now, but it has to do that better in the future. More importantly, "what is the one thing that I can do better than anyone else that won't only last a handful of years?"

This might be, "I am going to build the very best technical product that will help people of all descriptions to unlock incredible capabilities in themselves." If that's the case, then, again, you want that engineering function.

If it is a more service-based model, you might be thinking, 'I am going to help clients serve the entire planet. No one else is doing that. Everyone's serving themselves or serving a short-term need. I care so much about avoiding crises and solving the crises of the future that I'm going to help every single business also tackle those crises.' If you care about that, then how are you serving that client? With what people are you serving that client? Then you will want to get that function in-house.

This is where that first question needs to be answered pretty rigorously. What about your business that will last for decades? Do you hope to last for decades and last as the cream of the crop?

When you're identifying a function that you want in-house and what you want to accomplish is of significance, you'll quickly realize it is not a one-man endeavor. You are going to need others. As you think about the core reason for your entire company to exist and the vision you have that gets you excited about your business, wouldn't you want to put all of your absolute best and brightest into those functions? A classic truism of business applies here—If we're all rowing in the same direction, we can accomplish great things together.

You need to know what functions you want to row down. As soon as you realize what roles and functions you require for in-source talent support, you will quickly realize how much you need to involve others because you won't be able to fit every function into your schedule.

Articulate the Mission

The fallacy with vision, mission, and values is that, too often, they come from a business owner's ego. It shouldn't be like that. Your vision, mission, and values must be practical in the sense that it is feasible to accomplish a goal. And your goal is to get other people to buy into your company.

Now, it's fair to ask, 'Well, why do I have to do that? Why can't I just articulate what matters to me?' Here's the rub: It's already implicit that you, as the business owner and founder, have already bought into the company. You don't need to convince yourself twice.

What you need to do is to communicate it in a way that speaks to your individual employees and resonates with their own personal motivations, goals, and passions.

Keep in mind that employees can pretend and pay you lip service too. They'll say, "oh, yeah, great, cool, love your vision, love your mission." You must be able to see beyond that facade.

What you want is to see the light bulbs switch on and stir up a fire inside employees, where they start to have the same realizations you did. If you can ignite that spark inside them, you create a sense of urgency, and you inspire action.

Find & Attract A-Class Talent

Identifying A-class talent in today's world is not difficult. The problem lies in the dimensions that they are measured as A-class talent. This is where you will want to disrupt some of your own preconceived notions and conventional thinking. You don't want to hire based on their titles or locations. You don't even want to go on certain functions. When you're attracting A-class talent, you are going to want to look for people who have the ability to be resilient, show grit and be able to survive the troubles of decades to come.

Here are a few tips to find that A-class talent. Look for individuals who have had a diverse array of experiences and have done a little bit of everything. Someone who has weathered challenging circumstances, maybe a recession or two. Ironically enough, these are the types of candidates that might catch a red flag with traditional recruiters. Maybe look for someone who even has had an odd change of career or didn't stay in one industry for the course of their career. If you see someone who has systematically gone through their career, not only surviving, but thriving regardless of location, industry, and title, that says something about that person. It speaks volumes about their ability to succeed even when the chips are down.

You do not want talent that is merely excellent in one period of time. When you see someone who's had a fairly linear run of success, be cautious. That tells you that in certain environmental circumstances, they can succeed. But the second those environmental circumstances change, they may well not.

Don't look at who's done well in good times. Look at who's done well in bad times, because you know that the next crisis is just around the corner. Find talent that can accomplish great things, not just in the good, but also in the difficult times.

So that is finding the talent. How you attract them comes back to speaking the three languages we discussed. First, attract them financially. Take care of people's finances first so they don't have to worry about that. You don't need to pay them the top of the market price, but you need to be respectful enough to pay commensurate with their expertise. You also need to lay out a career plan for what they can accomplish with your company professionally.

But where you really need to dial in is in the personal, because this is where you are going to have a double-edged sword. You still want to have a diversity of thought, people's experiences, mindsets, and cultures because if you don't have these things, your business does not have agility and resilience, and groupthink is a single point of failure.

The challenge here for you is to figure out how to still attract the right people who are going to be personally invested in this decade-long vision. If your entire business hinges on these folks, you need to be vulnerable as a leader. Get out there, and through whatever mediums necessary, spread that message.

Not everyone who comes to you will be pure of heart. Some may be looking at your company as a stepping stone. Some will be looking at what they can take advantage of in that. You need to tighten up your grip as a discerning leader to figure out who, among the talent available, has come for the right reasons. And, as soon as you hire these individuals, the job doesn't stop there because now the clock is ticking. Can you match the promises you made?

The thing about A-class talent is that they will give you

less leeway because they are not with you to just collect a paycheck or a title. They care about doing something important, and they have a sense of urgency to make that happen, which makes them very precious with their time.

Measure Human Capabilities

When you're hiring, it is crucial to move away from the traditional measurement dimensions of the past such as technical knowledge and project-specific capabilities. Most companies focus on filling specific functions and are looking at this through a lens of, "I have a function that is missing and I need that function filled." But you are not creating a company purely based on function. You are creating a company that wants to leave a legacy and im-prove humanity. You want it to stand the test of time which means you need to fill roles that are not just based on one technical function.

Let's take the world of programming. If you have identified someone based on their years of experience in a particular programming language or framework, then it only takes a brand new language or framework to come two years from now, and that person's entire skill set is disrupted. To counter this, you need to scrutinize an individual beyond their project capabilities and instead look for their human capabilities. Project-specific capabilities of individuals are confined and limited insofar as they will only be useful in a matter of months or years, but they won't last beyond that.

I am not suggesting that "human capabilities" is just another word for "soft skills".

Soft skills are a given. While soft skills such as leadership, communication, and culture-fit are important, they are not the most critical factors for the long-term success of a company. For instance, culture-fit may not exactly be a reliable indicator because if your company is going to have the agility and the resilience to last decades, chances are, your company is going to change its culture quite a bit.

What do you really want to measure? What you really have to want to measure are the human capabilities that allow someone to succeed through the good and bad times across the decades. You will want to measure their willingness to learn, adaptability, critical thinking, and response to difficult circumstances. Do they get inspired to meet the challenge and rise to the occasion?

You can ask them questions about why they do what they do, and what excites them about joining the company and observe the words they use in response, how they respond, and their non-verbal cues. You should be able to see fairly definitively between someone who is just pretending and someone who is actively and emotionally vulnerable with you, who, therefore, can be honest with you. So that's the side of mindset.

On the side of the experience, you need to look at their past experiences rather than just relying on generic questions. Don't just ask, "tell me about how you performed your function. Tell me about the result." You have to really start digging into the areas where people had the most challenges in their life. Those are the areas you should focus on.

Did they undergo a significant shift in their industry? Did the person have a gap when they got laid off at some point and needed to make things work? Did they jump from a retail position because they had to do it just to put some food on the table, and then they managed to transition to something else? Did they have a side venture that they've developed in their own time?

Look at those areas where a traditional recruiter would say, "hm, that doesn't seem linear enough, and doesn't seem neatly in a box for me." There is a good chance those are the kind of people who have what it takes to endure and succeed in the long term. What you need to look for are individuals who faced numerous setbacks in life but have consistently bounced back and triumphed. Not only getting up to survive but getting up to ultimately thrive.

Set Them up for Success

The misconception in setting someone up for success is this

belief that because you've hired an expert in a particular function and let them work independently, it's enough to guarantee success.

This is a flawed approach for two key reasons: first, your business is always going to have its own idiosyncrasies and unique characteristics, and you need to make sure that you are aligning your people to those idiosyncrasies. This is something that a lot of business owners often tend to overlook. Second, bringing a function in-house requires more than just hiring an expert you have already deemed to be necessary for your long-term success. Why would you allow that team member to then dictate their own direction, where suddenly, if you multiply that across a couple of different functions, your business is then being pulled in multiple different directions?

The whole reason you decided to in-source this function was that there was something unique about this particular value offering that couldn't readily be systematized and turned into a component that could be outsourced. Therefore you need the people who fill that function to be crystal-clear aligned with what you are trying to create. Otherwise, you are going to inevitably disrupt the structure of your business and potentially lose out on the inbuilt resiliency and agility that you tried to build the business with at the very start.

It is important to make sure that you are not only setting up a person for success based on what your business is, but that you are also ensuring that they are being successful, not just for themselves, but for what your overall outcome is. Because it's not just about the cost that usually gets associated with a poor hire. You have to fire them, and you have to hire someone new; those things are table stakes and stock standards.

The cost here is that failing to set that person up for success can have a negative impact and disrupt your entire business structure. You need to rein in very clearly the direction of how your business continues to be built.

This is tricky because this is not advocating for micromanagement. Micromanagement will always kill any sort of gains that you might think you will yield out of it. You need to set up a culture, an 'operating system' if you will, that allows people to come in and be successful on their terms, but more importantly, on your business's terms.

The biggest challenge to your decision to even take on insourcing is the apprehension it creates. It can be daunting for business owners because you literally are taking on higher costs and taking on more fickle employees in many ways.

Those highly-skilled, A-class talents are critical to your business's function, and they know it. These people are some of the best that you will ever have, but for you as a business owner, they can be infuriating, because this is not going to be someone who will just put their head down and accept things blindly. They're going to have an opinion and they will say it. But as a smart business owner, you should recognize that you don't have all the answers.

And if you're going to rely on just yourself and outsource all your business's functions, then you will have a single point of failure.

We have talked at length about this idea, that for you to navigate the crises of the future, you cannot have single points of failure. Now you've agreed that you can't have a single point of failure in location. You've agreed you can't have a single point of failure in your business model. You've agreed you can't have a single point of failure in the industries that you serve.

We've talked at length about how you need to build agility and resilience to manage the next pandemic, the next war, the next supply chain crisis, all of these different aspects that will inevitably clash with your business and potentially cause it to go under. And you don't want that. You want it to last for decades to come.

But in order to do that, you need the mind power of not just yourself, but talented individuals as well.

That's why, even in the most distributed companies, you still need to in-source.

You still need to uncover what critical function cannot be done outside your company, the function that needs to implicitly and inherently be done on the inside, and you need to get the experts that can deliver on that.

Chapter 4

Outsourcing

Imagine if you could create a company where everyone is growing in the same direction, where everyone is working together to create a company that lasts for decades.

Imagine if you could create a truly prosperous company, a company that will see you earn untold riches and, more importantly, cement your legacy for years to come.

Getting people to connect to the vision and purpose of your business is the single greatest thing you can do for it. And one way you can do that is by outsourcing employees.

In order to begin outsourcing well, I am advocating that you outsource functions based on expertise.

The current state of outsourcing is still very much dictated around a couple of key areas. It's dictated around cost first and foremost, and it's dictated around subservience.

The first one, cost, is pretty self-explanatory. Cost is the initial reason that outsourcing was, in the 1980s, primarily based out of countries like India for functions such as call centers and customer support. For that reason, outsourcing was implicitly an exercise done by the finance team of companies. The thought process behind this was, 'let's not pay this customer support rep $50,000 a year in the U.S., let's pay someone $5,000 a year in Mumbai.'

But what was built into that concept was this idea of subservience, which is far more insidious and far more toxic. Indeed it's the reason that outsourcing, even to this day, has a horrid name. You ask many companies whether they have certain functions in-house, and what's their reaction? "No, we do it all ourselves." Companies go to great lengths to hide the fact that they outsource, and that should tell you everything you need to know about how they view it.

That is a real problem because, what have you created? You've created a pseudo-colonialistic business structure where you have the core country or the headquarters. Then you have the periphery or client states, i.e., the outsourced. And this creates a really bad imbalance in the business where the people at the top get to dictate to the outsourced function how to do their job.

What I'm advocating for, and what you need to start re-conceptualizing around outsourcing, is that you are going to outsource functions based on expertise. Yes, you might get some cost savings out of it, but that's not your idea. Your idea is not to get 10% less quality for 100% less cost. Your idea is to get 10% less cost and 100% improvement in quality.

That is how outsourcing, when done correctly, can yield much for your business. You can take advantage of a talent pool that isn't based on the first world, second world, or third world, but a unified globe where talent can exist anywhere and talent for different functions can exist anywhere.

So rather than being dictatorial about how you decide your business operates from the top, you need to look at how you can build your business to serve its different outsourced functions. How can you maximize the structure to accommodate those areas of outsourcing to yield maximum success? Your goal is not only to reap the benefits of the best possible talent across the world, but in a way that preserves the flexibility and agility of your business so that you continue to get the best talent.

As we know, across the world, some pretty bad phenomena are happening that pose a huge risk for businesses, none more so than aging populations. And what does that mean? If you think you're in a talent war right now, you're going to be in a hell of a talent war in five to ten years' time.

So then, why would you restrict yourself? Why would you mandate how things are going to be done? Why would you not go and find the best possible talent and make sure you are serving them to do the best possible work for you. That's the power of outsourcing.

The first step is very critical. You've already decided what to insource; now you're doing the same exercise for out-sourcing. Which functions are defined enough?

If the key idea about insourcing was that we were looking at the less well-defined functions that are critical to your business, now we are going to need more flexibility.

We're looking at outsourcing to be the best possible function that have clear definitions and that have clear criteria for success. Have you thought about that for your business? That's the first step.

Once you've decided on the functions that need to be out-sourced, then the next step is talent sourcing. This is where you look to the globe. For example, you've decided you're going to outsource your software development. You need to now think of a couple of key things. One, the nature of your business that relates to how you need this function to work, and two, where is the best possible talent?

So continuing to use software development as an example, you might look at onshore America, Latin America, or Eastern Europe. You might look through all those things and see those different areas and determine who is the best in terms of quality, in terms of code standards, in terms of velocity. But then you might also think, 'do I need this to be done in sync with my existing team?'

'I might want to have them be in a similar region to me. Do I need it to be 24 hours? In which case I want people all over the globe. I want them in different time zones.'

Is cost the only consideration? I would argue no. You need to be looking at who builds the best for what you need. But you can't just go to the best, full stop. It's not just about being the highest possible quality; it's about being the highest possible quality for your specific business. That's the second step.

The third step, once we've sourced the region and the talent, is figuring out the model. This is what I would call the legal ramifications, because different countries have different ways. Yes, right now, in the year we are in, it's easier than ever to hire anyone from all around the globe. But you need to recognize that there are still going to be a few regulatory hurdles. Those hurdles need to be considered.

How do I need to employ someone? Do I need to make them a contractor? Am I allowed to make them a contractor? What is the expectation of talent in a particular region?

Do they expect certain benefits? Do they have certain vacation policies they expect? Those types of things also need to be factored into your decision-making.

The fourth step is to make a compelling offer. You have set up your business to succeed. You have set up your business to last for decades. You need to now articulate that same vision to your outsourced team. You might think that 'Oh, I've already done it with the insourced team, I don't need to bother. I've already got a clearly defined process, a clearly defined function for my outsource team, so we don't need to do that.'

Wrong. You absolutely have to do that. Because if your outsourced functions have the same binding to your vision and mission, and values, the same buy-in to what you're trying to create, then they will go above and beyond for you. This isn't just a commercial transaction. We are trying to build a business that can survive some of humanity's greatest crises, crises that we are about to face in the near future.

If you can build a business with a level of respect for your talent, regardless of whether they're insourced or outsourced, it will benefit you. Because those are the people you want buying into your company.

You don't want an outsourced person who's just taking this as a job, who's just taking this for a paycheck. You want them committed so that you have insourced and outsourced talent working together as one team.

And then, finally, once you have made that offer and you have brought those people into your company, you will want to be setting them up for success as well.

Because yes, when you've outsourced a function, you have a clearly defined set of metrics. You have a clearly defined process. You have a clearly defined function that they are fulfilling. Whether it's back office, whether it's software development, whether it's design, whether it's accounting, whatever that function is that is clearly defined. That is why you've outsourced it.

They will have their own ideas on their own success metrics, but once again, this is not about letting the entire company decide their own success metrics; it's about defining what is success for you, for your business.

How do you align your outsourced teams to achieve success, not just in the project they're doing today, but the projects they do in the future to contribute to your overall decades-long vision? That is the key here. We are trying to create a business that will survive all sorts of shocks to the system. And if your teams can help you survive those disruptions, then your outsourced team and your insourced team should have cohesively, together, driven the business result that you are ultimately aiming for.

Crystalize Functions

This is where a lot of legwork needs to be done, because when you've insourced a function, you can, by definition, be a little more vague. You can have the subject matter expert partially dictate how that function is created. But in order to achieve success with outsourcing, in order to find the talent that is going to be appropriate for the function, you need to have a very clear idea of what a function accomplishes.

So let's take an example of an accounting team. Are you using an accounting team to merely make sure that your people get paid on time? Are you using an accounting team merely to ensure that business expenses and business income is tracked? Are you trying to get more complicated parts? Are you trying to get certain tax advantages? Are you trying to set up your business in a way that is able to be nimble in terms of how it's set up, where it's set up, where it's located, and do you have answers to all of these questions?

You can apply the same methodology across your product building. You can apply the same methodology across service offerings; you can apply the same methodology across systems, processes, back office staff, marketing staff, and sales staff.

Making sure that you have clear definitions in place early

will allow you to go into the following steps and do that successfully. If you don't have a clear idea of what you are trying to achieve out of a particular function, what you are likely going to end up doing is just burning cash. You're going to hire the wrong way.

This is a classic human trait. When humans have no other information to make a decision on, what do you think is the one dimension they make their decision based on? Price. And that is not what you want to land yourself in. You can still factor it in, but if you don't have clear definitions, your mind is going to conspire against you and make you only choose based on price. That compromises your business's ability to succeed enormously. Because, as we know, price is not indicative of value. It just isn't. It's one way, but it ain't the only way.

So, you need to crystalize those functions to figure out what exactly needs to happen in them. Building that perfect vision, you know, ask yourself the question about a function. 'In a year from now, in 5 years from now, in 10 years from now, what do I hope this function achieves? What would a successful employee in this function look like? Painting that vision for yourself will give you a clear idea of the next steps of who you need to hire, where you need to hire them, and even why you need to hire them.

Talent Sourcing

Once you've figured out exactly the level of expertise, the level of proficiency you need, and, more importantly, what and why a particular function is contributing to your business, you can start to talent-source. You now need to think across a range of dimensions when thinking about getting that talent in.

You need to start first and foremost with quality. Quality is always the best way. There is a phenomenon within most industries, indeed with most humans, that when systems are left untouched, the vast majority of benefits accrue to the top. You can see this happen in industries. There's always a big four, a big five, a big six, but not much more than that. Why is that? It's because when companies dominate a space, similar to when humans dominate a space, they get far more learnings, outsized learnings, and impact compared to the majority.

Now we can debate whether this is a good thing or not, but it is a phenomenon of nature. Because it is a phenomenon of nature, it is always a good idea to use quality as your first metric. As much as you can anticipate the benefits when you hire the best possible talent for their function, you will get unrealized benefits, and particularly, unrealized benefits that compound over time.

You, Mr. or Ms. Business Owner, are probably familiar

with the eighth wonder of the world, compound interest. But what if I told you that everything in life compounds, particularly if you are hiring the best possible talent, their knowledge, their expertise and their innovation compounds over time. If you're looking to keep your business going for decades, imagine what that compounding effect could do for you.

First, look at quality. But then, beyond quality, you need to look at the semantics. You need to look at how your business engages with all of itself day to day, because this comes down to a logistical challenge. It is not enough to merely have the best possible talent. You need to make sure you have the best possible talent that can serve your particular business model.

So, for example, if you're in a client service model, then it doesn't do well to have team members that are not overlapping with a client's time zone. You need to have that because it is service related. Are you in a product business where your product can be built independently? Then perhaps you don't need that. Perhaps asynchronous communication will better serve you.

Thinking through both the first part, which is the quality of the talent that you're sourcing, but more importantly, how that matches the unique logistical considerations of your business, is paramount. At the end of the day, you need to accrue the benefits of the best talent for your organization. And that is only going to happen if people are set up for the really mundane. I think it's as mundane as it gets. How people communicate with one another in your organization.

Because we know the evil of silos. As soon as your different functions are not speaking to one another and not communicating regularly, you don't have a business; you have a series of independent functions. How can you gain that elusive synergy, like "one plus one equals three," if all you have is a bunch of independent silos. They may as well be independent companies at that point.

So first think of the quality, but then think of logistics.

Make a Compelling Offer

When you think of bringing on an outsourced function, your temptation is to drill into their expertise. And business owners often do this. They often put their outsourced functions through the rigger far more often than they do with their own in-house employees. They sometimes hold their outsourced functions to a higher standard than their in-house employees. And they do this because there is a level of certainty. They think that because it is easy to define, therefore it is easy to measure.

But the problem with starting a conversation with someone who is going to be outsourced is it immediately puts it into transactional terms. You are subtly and subconsciously communicating to that person on the other side, "I only see you as what you can achieve for me in terms of a project, in terms of a function, in terms of an outcome." And as any good business owner such as yourself would know, that is not a way to build a business. When people feel like they're a number, when people aren't connected to a broader purpose, they are immediately only going to put in the effort that is required to meet that expectation. It is just a pure transaction to them.

So what is the risk here? The risk is that they are only going to give you 51% of effort. We know the problem of that in terms of disengaged employees, but how about outsourced employees, outsourced contractors? What happens there? That means they don't come to you with a new idea. They don't suggest an innovation. They don't tell you what they're seeing in the market. They just do their particular project, and that's it. Nothing more, nothing less.

Compare on the other hand, if you started your introduction with that outsourced employee by talking to them about what you were trying to create, how you were trying to build that vision for a better world, and how you were practically delivering on that promise.

How you're building a company that can last for decades, that can provide gainful employment, that can help change the trajectory, not just of your small region, but regions around the world.

Imagine the power of their creativity and innovation when they know that they are contributing to a truly global enterprise, and a global enterprise for good. If they are connected to that, then the overflow of benefits you will receive are immense because it's not just about them being able to perform their function correctly; it's about them being able to bring new innovations, new suggestions, new ways of performing their function even better. Because everyone has it.

You've hired them, or are trying to hire them, because of their expertise in their function. Anyone who is an expert in their function has ideas, and keeps their finger on the pulse of what is happening.

But do you want them to keep that to themselves and pursue their own business with their ideas? Or would you prefer to show that you holistically care about them, regardless of the fact that they are outsourced? If you can demonstrate that care, those ideas won't be hidden away by your outsourced contractors. They will be brought to you, and your business will gain the benefit of it.

Talent Sensitivity

So when we think about talent sensitivity, we're really rejecting colonialism in all its forms. Let's just do a quick history lesson.

As we go through the ages, power, and specifically asymmetric power, has been a theme of humanity since the very beginning. We look at the pharaohs of Egypt and the immense power they wielded compared to their subordinates. We look at the lords and barons of the middle ages and the serfs that served them. And then, even once we started seeing rising incomes in the West, we just took those same toxic systems and applied them across the world. We were able to pacify the working classes in the West in exchange for outsourcing their functions to more subservient regions of the world.

This is not a way to conduct business. Because every single person has a core expertise. Everyone has a lived experience that allows them to have a unique perspective on the world. And that unique perspective is inherently valuable. So, Mr. Business Owner, don't merely decide that everything is viewed through your own cultural lens, your own lived experience. You need to tap into the lived experiences and the expectations of your talent by truly showing you value each person as an individual.

Now we can all talk the big talk about building company culture, but to a lot of people, that's fairly fluffy. So to have true talent sensitivity, you want to demonstrate it in concrete terms. That means understanding local customs. That means understanding local communication styles.

How someone prefers to communicate in one region of the world can substantially differ from another. Understanding the cultural norms such as festivals, holidays, and vacations, making sure that you're aware of those regardless of where your talent is located. Because it doesn't take much to give someone a holiday for their own cultural festival. But when you demonstrate that, especially compared to the colonialistic attitudes of many companies that engage in outsourcing, you are going to see unparalleled results. You're going to see your outsourced functions really take notice that you value them as individuals, as humans.

And beyond that, remember that every unique individual, when they're undertaking employment, has an idea of what they should be contributing. They have an idea of how to do it. You are trying to build a picture of corporations for the future. You are trying to build a corporation that doesn't just look at the next quarterly profit, but truly lasts for decades. And if you're trying to do that, then you need to show not only adherence, but also acceptance of how people work.

You need to show them that you are willing to put your own ideas, your own preconceived notions, to the side and interact with each of them on an individual level. When you do that, you demonstrate significant care. And when that happens, while you might feel like it is a lot of effort, I can promise you it repays itself 10 times, 100 times over, because you cannot deny the reality that we live in. Most outsourced functions have an imbalance of power. What would the world look like if you rebalanced it?

Set Your Employees up for Success

So, once again, you've attracted employees with your vision, mission, and values. You've identified that your talent is going to be of sufficient quality. You've identified how you are going to maximize the potential of this talent, and you've told them, and demonstrated to them through clear actions, that you care about them.

Now they're on board, you need to make sure they're successful. And making sure they're successful is not just about hitting KPIs for their particular function. That's obvious; that's implicit. In many ways, it should be even easier, because your outsourced functions should have clear ideas of KPIs that will measure their impact. What you need to do is thread the needle of those KPIs towards the broader vision. You need to show them how what they're contributing is not only successful for them, but it's actually driving the company forward. When you do that, then you're able to really communicate this idea that you, holistically, as a business, care about them, regardless of whether they're insourced or outsourced.

You are playing a longer-term game. You are playing an infinite game.

When you are playing that infinite game, you are contributing to a company that is looking to change the world. Making sure those success metrics are set up to align with what your business is trying to accomplish is paramount because, at the end of the day, it's not going to be hard to measure the success.

You will be able to get through several project runs. You might even be able to get through several years with outsource functions, fairly implicitly, hitting their KPIs each quarter. That's not your problem with an outsourced function. Your problem is when they become disillusioned. Your problem is when they start feeling roboticized when they just feel like what they're doing is arbitrary numbers, when they feel like what they're doing doesn't matter.

As your organization shifts and changes, your talent will be creative and innovative. Bringing those qualities to your organization and allowing them to flourish will be important so that you can truly succeed, so that they can succeed, and hopefully, the world can succeed.

Outsourcing has had a bad rap for its entire existence, and you're going to continue to give it a bad rap if you follow the sins of the past because, at the end of the day, a short-term game on cost or control is not worth it.

You need to dispense with that idea, especially control, because in today's business landscape, you are going to have increasingly less control over the circumstances of the world.

You're not going to be able to control the next outbreak. You're not going to be able to control the next war or supply chain issues, food shortages, or water crises. You can't control any of that, and so assuming that you can control your business in the same way is just a pure fallacy.

Don't fall for the sins of the past. Don't treat your outsourced functions as numbers, because they know that they're humans too. They have feelings, hopes, desires, aspirations, and they want what we all want. They want to do something that matters, and they want to contribute to making a world that is better when they leave it than it was when they entered it. You can give them that.

You have already shown an aptitude for a global enterprise. A global enterprise is very unique because you are trying to create something that is universal, that is inherently human. Something that is not localized and is based on our species.

When you can reject the sins of outsourcing, when you can reject its colonialistic tendencies, the idea that it is a cost-based measure and nothing else, you are able to start to create a company that will actually serve this world and serve this planet for the better.

Ultimately, if you do that, you are the one who is going to prosper, because everyone who's been thinking in short-term gain and in exploitation terms, is going to have both a series of crises they'll face from outside, and crises from within. Because when you treat people as numbers, when you treat them just as cogs in a machine, they'll work against you. You might not realize how much they work against you, but they do.

Go across your entire business. You've already done the exercise for insourcing. Therefore, everything that you haven't insourced, implicitly, you have decided can be made clear; it should be very self-evident. If it can be made clear, then it can be outsourced.

List those functions out. Let's just make sure that you have very clear functions, whether it's accounting, back office, or product engineering, list all of them out. Once you've listed all of them out, you need to go into each of them and paint an ideal final outcome. You need to do that first before we go and source the location, because we need the location and the talent to match the ideal outcome.

Do a small exercise, one year from now and five years from now. One year is short-term enough. Five years is long-term enough, but not too long that it becomes abstract.

Write out what you hope a function has achieved in one year from now and five years from now.

For talent sourcing, you now need to go across a matrix. The first step you want to look at is quality. Where are the best possible quality talents for this particular function that you have identified?

How do you find that information? You can look in trade publications and search on social media. Social media is a really good one for this because many people have lots of opinions. You can aggregate those opinions. You can lean on particular industry experts and see what they say about particular talents.

Once you've identified particular regions, that's when you want to start engaging with recruiters, especially region-specific recruiters. If you've already done the legwork upfront of figuring out what region someone should be in, then you want to use people who know that talent market best.

You've done the hard work. Let the experts do the next part.

Once again, this is where you're going to get a double whammy. Those same recruiters who are going to help you source the talent should also be able to start giving you a picture of what it means to have talent sensitivity.

They will give you advice on the cultural ramifications of your chosen location. You can also learn from broader experts here and consult with a professional employment organization, or PEO. These are global organizations that help you hire people across the world in various different regions.

You are going to get a lot of cultural information just by searching online. One of the inherent curiosities of human nature Is that we're very interested in people from different backgrounds and different cultures. You can deal with that side of it yourself.

The legal and HR side of it? Definitely tap those experts. You can partly use the recruiters that you are going to engage with but you can also use broader organizations to just inform how you should make offers to people. How do people expect to be employed by a particular organization?

That compelling offer really starts with you. First and fore-most, it's not just about putting an offer package together that has a base salary, incentives, and benefits. That's all stock standard. But, have you gained the excitement? Have you compellingly made a case so that someone can see themselves in your company?

You're going to have to be very discerning with this. You're going to have to subvert your usual way of asking questions because you're not going to just regurgitate a vision.

You're not just going to talk about your talent for 30 minutes or an hour.

You, CEO, need to listen. You need to find what that intrinsic motivation is within your talent. You need to make sure that intrinsic motivation matches with what you're trying to accomplish, and you need to effectively communicate to ensure that what the individual wants to accomplish is the same as what you want to accomplish.

When you find talent that matches that dimension, that's when you're going to succeed.

Make sure that you set up, if not day one, at least within the first month, to show the talent your broad company goals and an insight into how their work can contribute to those company goals. This is not just an exercise of goal setting. This is making sure that no matter what function you are employing at any one time, they are always aware of what your North Star is.

Keeping with what an outsourced function is doing whilst ensuring it's connected to a broader purpose, not just for the individual but for the company at large, is critical. Because when you can do that, your outsourced functions will last much longer than a project timeline, even longer than a milestone sprint; they will last for decades.

It's very easy here to just lean on vision and mission, but that doesn't feel very concrete to people. You need to pull it back down to, "what are we accomplishing this year?" You need to tailor that conversation based on different functions.

If you're speaking to someone in a revenue function, that's pretty straightforward. You give them a revenue number, and you say, "this is what I'm trying to accomplish this year, can you help me?" You don't put it all on them. You take ownership, because that's why you're CEO.

Similarly, if you're speaking to someone completely different in product, perhaps you want to talk in terms of "here's what I'm hoping to achieve from user satisfaction with our product."

Figure out which of those North Stars will motivate your function in the most compelling way. When you do that, you are setting them up to accomplish what you want them to do, and they will do the rest of the work. They will figure out the 'how,' and they will figure out the 'what' in terms of communicating that effectively to customers and to stakeholders.

If you've articulated how the North Star matches to each individual, you're setting them up to take your vision and mission and push your company forward.

This is what outsourcing is really about.

Chapter 5

Sourcing Structure

I've heard a variation of this so many times. "I grew up in a major metropolitan area, and I worked in a major metropolitan area ... That's the way I've always done business. So that's how I should set up my business."

I believe that when we look at how businesses work today, the biggest problem is that businesses keep building their models based on their owner's personalities.

Even if your company is small, chances are that you will be serving customers across your country and across the globe. With very few exceptions, most of your commerce is going to rely on this.

At the core of "how do I grow revenue?," is a question you need to ask yourself. Do you serve a large body of customers with a low-value offering, or do you serve a low number of customers with a high-value offering?

In both of those cases, you cannot restrict yourself to a single location, because if you're serving the maximum number of customers possible, by definition, you are going to be global. You're going to try and start from your country of residence, and then you're going to try and increasingly expand from that because if your business serves a low-value offering, then many people can afford it right across the world.

Similarly, if it's a high-value offering and there's only a handful of people who can be customers, then why would you assume that those people are going to be in one location? They're not all going to be in one city. They'll be, at the very least, in a handful of cities.

When we start to conceptualize that in terms of revenue, we think about our cost structure. You think about your operating expenses, but at the end of the day, you must answer the question of why did you get into business? You got into business because you thought there was a problem that you could solve better than anyone else.

If you do solve it better than anyone else, you will receive the reward. The reward, in our contemporary society, is money, and so given that, and given that you are now increasingly competing against not just other companies in your city, but you're competing for customers across the globe, then why would you not also want to take advantage of distributed structures?

You will want to take advantage of distributed structures for many of the reasons that we've already talked about. You'll be able to source and obtain the best possible talent from anywhere, but you'll also be able to gain a further understanding of your customer base.

When you bring in these disparate perspectives, when you're able to create your business model across a wide lens of demographics, location, mindset, personalities, and all of that, it culminates in a business that is able to see the opportunities and see the writing on the wall.

We've talked at length in this book about the crises that are going to happen, and we talk a lot about some of the more recent crises that have happened that "no one could have predicted." I would argue that this thinking is flawed.

You can always see some level of crisis before it happens. If you have enough data points and if you have enough expertise within your organization, that will allow you to see disruptions before they happen.

Let's use the example of the Covid-19 pandemic. Everyone says, "no one could have seen the pandemic." But the fact of the matter is, we do know where it started. It started in China. Early on, in late 2019, there was a virus. We did not know that it was going to proliferate into this global phenomenon, but we did know it existed.

How did we know it existed? Because we are tapped into a globalized world. And if you can adopt that same mentality for your business rather than restrict yourself to one city or one country, where suddenly these external factors are going to come in and catch you off guard, you'll have people who can alert you like, "hey, this thing is on the horizon." And as we know, in business, every risk has another side of the coin–an opportunity.

Again, going back to the pandemic example–yes, it was an awful, awful thing for humanity. Widespread illness. Yet, there were businesses that profited from it. There were medical advancements. There were advances in personal protection equipment.

There were advances in technology solutions that allowed us to do things remotely, and allowed supply chains to be supported.

There's always an opportunity to serve a need; that's why you got into business. And so, wouldn't you want the structure of your business to mimic that reason so that you can always be ready to serve the next great opportunity?

I think the first structure needed for businesses is a revenue model. So are you trying to service the entire globe, or are you trying to serve a particular segment within different pockets of the globe? That will dictate how you set it up.

The second structure determines how interconnected you will need to be with different opportunities. If you're going to create a business right now that lasts decades into the future, you will always have to adapt to new changing environments in order to continue to be relevant.

You cannot build a business in one ecosystem anymore because one only has to look at Moore's law, which states that technology doubles every 18 months, and that is only going to increase the disruption to economies. So then you need to ask yourself, what is your core business? How can you create something that's universal?

The third structure determines how you are trying to match your employees to the clientele that you serve.

If you're serving clients all over the world, then you should have corresponding employees to those clients. If we're looking at the entrenched advantages for organizations that will go into the future, it's going to be the people who implicitly understand their customers.

This is not just superficial stuff like knowing who your customers are, their net worth, their lifestyle stage, and all the usual marketing metrics that people look at. You're going to have to know them really deeply. You're going to have to know every one of your customers so intrinsically that you know their thoughts, their hopes and dreams, and how they conceptualize the world. Because when you can do that, you again, go back to the core—if you understand someone so completely, you understand their problems. If you understand their problems, you can serve them a solution that meets their needs.

I still think there's something to be said for matching your employee base to your customer from a personality, location, and cultural aspect. I think what I'm trying to get at with that idea specifically, is that you'll be able to do a process known as "client cloning."

In order to grow globalized, you need to serve a need, and the need needs to be large enough that there's enough people willing to pay for it. If you have customers all over the globe and you have employees that understand those customers more intrinsically than anyone else, then suddenly, you are able to clone those customers right across the world in each of their own little markets.

You can't do that if you are committing some of the sins that we've talked about before, like just being focused on one area or one country and exporting it in a colonialistic fashion. You need 'boots on the ground.'

This goes back to our previous two chapters. It doesn't matter whether those people are insourced or outsourced; you just need the people. You can figure out the best model to employ those people, but you need them in order to build that inherent flexibility into your business model and, more importantly, the resilience. Because as soon as you're only serving one type of customer or one type of industry or one type of country, you are subject to its risks.

You only have to look at one example: the hospitality industry, a very successful industry, hit 2020, and companies lost 90-95% of their revenue overnight.

Those types of crises, as we've talked about at length in this book, are only going to continue to happen. And so if they're going to continue to happen, you will want as much resiliency as possible built into your business from the get-go. The best way to get that resiliency is to serve as many different types of people as possible. By serving those different types of people, you'll be alert to those opportunities.

Employees build the resiliency of a business to allow its vision to be actualized.

If you've done those first four steps, what you're ultimately building is a structure of a business that can achieve impact, but even more importantly, global impact.

And why will you want to do that? Not just because it's a nice thing.

It is, of course, a nice thing. We all want meaning, and

business owners, in particular, often talk about a grander purpose and a grander vision, which is all conceptualized around impact. But it's even more important to realize that it's only companies driven by impact that last decades.

A classic example here is Apple. Apple, right now, whilst it builds the iPhone, is not just a smartphone manufacturer. They have services that will obviously take over their hardware sales in a pretty short space of time.

Nike, as another classic example, doesn't just sell shoes.

Look at the companies that are able to command the zeitgeist of an entire population of people. Those are the types of companies that can survive a change in everything we've talked about. They can survive a change in the revenue model. They can survive a change in operating structure, and they can survive supply chain collapses.

All of these different aspects become the semantics of running a business in service of that greater impact-driven vision.

●　●

Resiliency tends to be talked about in terms of natural disasters. I know that resiliency functions within companies are building plans in case of nuclear attacks and the rest of it. Yes, that's catastrophic, but it's not really why we're trying to build resiliency here.

We're trying to build resiliency because we know that change is always a constant. And so, even if the change that happens to your business isn't catastrophic, you'll still need resiliency inherent to it in order to continue to serve your customers' needs.

I think it's as simple as that; you just don't want to bet on one horse.

Revenue Model

I think the first decision that needs to be made with your revenue model really comes down to that first binary choice . Are you looking to serve a large number of people with an affordable offering? Or are you looking to serve a small number of people with a very expensive offering? Is it somewhere in between?

What that will dictate is where you start. Because as you can imagine, with any of these revenue models, it takes time to build momentum, So if you're trying to build that momentum, you need to think of the easiest place for you to first serve customers.

Inherently, businesses that tend to survive over time accumulate more and more resources. That's why you're trying to make this last for decades. But everyone starts from somewhere, and that somewhere is zero.

What you need to think about first and foremost with this revenue model that you're constructing, is if you are trying to target a very specific person with a very specific need.

If that's the case, then you need to deploy your resources to serve that need, both human resources and capital resources, and you need to understand everything about the customer.

Or are you trying to serve a broader, more general human need?

Those two binaries are very simple to think about. If you serve a more expensive offering, it's likely more specific and more unique to an individualized human and an individualized group of humans with similar characteristics.

If you are serving a large body of people, then that large body of people is going to have fewer common traits. So those common traits are going to cause you to need a more broad human aspect in your business.

From there, once you're thinking about that first binary decision of what the product or service is, whether it's expensive or affordable, you will want to look at identifying where an initial sample of your customers are.

If they are very specific, then you will want to do a little bit of initial research to see how many different people fit that category.

Is it realistic to serve all of those needs? If so, where do you need your people to be placed in order to realize that actual revenue?

However, if you're thinking broadly about serving a large number of people, then you need to think about who's going to pick up your product or service the fastest.

If there is a broad enough variety of people, then the quickest way you need to get to some form of revenue is by deciding who within the general population would be an early adopter of your solution. Then you can start to build your momentum from there.

Opportunity Identification

If you've built your revenue model and you've started to see some particular traction, opportunity identification presents itself in two ways. You either double down on an area where you have served a particular client base or a particular customer base. You can get additional revenue that way, but you don't want to do it too much.

Why is that? Because once again, you are pigeonholing yourself towards being disrupted in future crises.

In order to get opportunities for the future, you need to now look at what you are creating in your product or service that is serving the needs of your existing revenue. Could that be taken to a completely different market, to a completely different industry, or to a completely different section of the globe?

If you can do that, then suddenly, you will start to build agility within your business model. Suddenly you'll be building components into your business that will allow you to think, 'hey, if some of our revenue goes, we have this other part that won't be disrupted.'

Play out a few scenarios in your head. Start to think about, 'hey, if tomorrow I lost all of this revenue from this entire service line, what would pick up the slack?' When you start to think in those terms, then you can start to identify what the opportunities will yield.

You cannot pick this all yourself. No individual has the sum of all knowledge. You need to be a contrarian to yourself. Find the people, find the locations, find the mindsets, the markets where people think in a completely different way. If you can find those people, that's where your talent should reside.

Suddenly you're going to build more and more flexibility into your model. It's not a bad thing to have gotten some success with a particular revenue model, but if you're going to last, you cannot just focus on it.

This is the number one cardinal sin that most companies do. Once they see a little bit of traction, they just focus on that and ignore everything else. And that's why companies die, even successful companies.

Companies can reach many millions of dollars in revenue

and then fail and fade into obscurity. They do that because they only serve one type of need and one type of problem. As soon as that problem goes away, as soon as that problem is solved by a better solution, suddenly the business model that you've come up with, that you thought was rock solid, is on much more shaky ground.

Co-Location

This is the biggest benefit of diversity for your organization. Everyone talks about diversity in moral terms. "We're bringing people together from different backgrounds, with different mentalities and different mindsets, that's a good thing," but why should you care? You're in business. You care about the economic impacts.

The most important thing that comes from building that diversity into your organization is implicitly understanding different customer bases. How are you, from the solitary individual perspective that you have accumulated, going to do that?

You cannot know all of the intricacies of every single one of your clients, or of every single market that you serve. So, this is where you need to build that type of co-location.

It's not just simple enough to build diversity; this is a fallacy. You don't want to just build diversity for diversity's sake. It's not just enough to hire women and hire minorities. Because a person who is based in one specific location, regardless of what their demographic and psychographic data is, is unique to that location.

You need to think across a wide spectrum. You need to think about who the different groups are in the different markets that you serve. Do you serve a particular class level? We don't like to talk a lot about class in America, but it is just as important, if not more important, than the usual dimensions we talk about, like race, gender, and sexuality.

You need to start building that cross-section–a cross-section of people that implicitly understand.

And in order to implicitly understand, one of the easiest things to do is diversify your location. Why location? Because it's about shared experience. People in a particular environment, with a particular set of circumstances, will have shared experiences similar to one another.

We talk all the time about the different characteristics of different cities. We talk about different characteristics of different countries; we talk about the different characteristics of urban versus rural living. All of those apply.

Why do they apply? Because our environment affects us. We're not just solitary beings that stay the same from day one. Our environment inherently shapes us, so acknowledging that and building that into your company is critical.

Now you might, as we've talked about in the previous chapters, find it easier for certain functions that are domestically based to you, to be insourced. You might want the functions that are overseas to be outsourced. That doesn't matter here. What matters is making sure that you have the right people in the right place to serve the right people with the right product.

Don't Bet on One Horse

One only has to look at one of the biggest fallacies that you, Mr. Business Owner, have received from very poor marketers. Who has told you, at length, that you need to niche down and that you need to focus on a niche? To that, I would say, look at the biggest company in the world.

Does Coca-Cola only serve people who like sugar? Does Apple only serve the wealthiest individuals? Does Nike only focus on one sport? None of them do, because each of them understands that in order to last for decades, you cannot have a single point of failure.

You never want to bet on that solitary horse. You can ride it; you can do it for one year, three years, five years, you can do it to an exit. That's fine.

As we've talked about, you're not building for an exit. You're building for legacy. You're building to last, and if you're building to last, you need to think about how you can build different products and services and have them ready.

You don't necessarily need every product and service to

be a huge success, but you need to build those revenue models. Why? Because as soon as one product or service gets disrupted and you've bet on one horse, that's your business gone.

We always talk about how "cash is king" in the world of business. You need the cash flows in order to survive any crisis, and as we've talked about, there's going to be a lot of them to survive.

Rather than wait and have that one product or service that will inevitably get disrupted, why wouldn't you be building multiple products or services? Contingency plans, if you will. Because as much as every business owner likes to pretend that what they do is somehow unique, it's not. There are ideas, themes, and self-concepts within a product or service that are applicable to people right across the world. You might think that what you offer is super individualized or super tailored, but the fact is, humans have many of the same basic needs.

Even if we look at most companies, they're serving, at their core, ideas around growing for the future. Helping people live better, more convenient lives, helping them with their happiness, helping them with their health, helping them with their finances.

These core ideas are universal. They've existed as long as homo sapiens have been a species. We might have changed the way we deliver those products and services to people, we might have added a lot more technology, but those core needs, those core problems we're solving, they're the same now as when we were just hunter-gatherer tribes.

They're the same as when we first started building farms and collecting grain. That hasn't changed. And that doesn't change fast. That's evolution. That changes over millions and millions of years.

Therefore, given that, why would you not look very hard at where you've got success and think, 'how can I take what I've learned here about making money? Because clearly, if I'm making money right now, I'm solving a problem and serving a need that people will pay me for.'

'How can I translate that to other markets, other types of people, and through that process, start to build different offerings, different products, all of which have their own market they're serving, their own need they're addressing. Through the accumulation of all of those efforts, my business is now no longer relying on one and maybe not even two.'

Maybe it's three, four, five, et cetera, et cetera. As that builds, suddenly, your business can handle a shock to the system. It's ready for the next opportunity. It's ready to last.

So-Called Impact

Impact is one of those words that is just a trope at this point. It's used over and over again. It's often used to hide more nefarious dealings, and sometimes it's used as greenwashing or another form of corporate propaganda, but you don't have to care about that.

You just got into business to make some money. And if you did, why did you make money? You made money because you solved problems, and if you solve big enough problems, you make a lot of money.

But when you've built your business in this way, in this distributed fashion, where you're serving the needs of many different people, many different locations, and many different countries, you incidentally will create a global impact.

It's not necessarily about starting with that. You don't need to delude the masses with some cult of personality about how you are the world's savior.

You can just simply focus on the core fundamentals of what you do best. You're trying to build a business that lasts, and you're trying to build a business that won't be disrupted by crises. You're trying to build a business that has inherent resiliency. If you're building with those things in mind, you cannot help but create an impact.

You're going to inevitably impact people right across

the world because you're serving talent right across the world. You're solving problems right across the world, and through the amalgamation of those, you inevitably are creating a business that not only lasts, but a business that is a positive force for good.

That is the type of business that we need right now, because we're done. Humanity cannot afford another set of businesses that are extractive and exploitative. We're on our last legs, and our planet won't survive that, but if you take this idea and create a business that will truly change the world, you will create the impact that we hope can be realized from the concept of a company.

Humans are receptive to that idea. We've wanted it. There's a reason that brands that serve customers to this day are beloved. They're beloved because they serve and solve problems that people have in their everyday lives. Wouldn't you want your brand, your company, to be one of those?

You need to think in terms of two aspects. I won't call it a shortterm; I'll call it a medium-term and a long-term.

The medium term is very simple for you. You are building a business that will survive the increasing level of crises and the increasing level of disruption that is going to happen. You're going to profit, and you'll profit quite well.

Maybe it'll be a little bit, or maybe you'll make a lot of money. You're able to create a business that doesn't have a large body of operating expenses, that is able to serve people right around the world and gain revenue from right around the world. That's nice, that's fun, and we can all build a business like that.

But if you do what is prescribed here, what you are going to create is a company that not only lasts, but can also be beloved. That is critical at this point in time that we're at. We're at a point in time where we need companies to step up. We need companies to show us the way, to prove to us that we, as a species, can overcome our failings. That is what the promise is on offer.

Governments aren't going to do that. They are too locked into their cycles. Individual humans are not going to do it because, unfortunately, individual humans are beholden to their own interests in a very short-term capacity. They've still got to put food on the table, and they've still got to put a roof over their heads. They can only respond, and even the most proactive people will tend to merely respond to crises.

So, look at it all. Across the board, what structure could we come up with that could last? It's not governments it's not individual people, it's not infrastructure. Infrastructure crumbles, and infrastructure decays. The only things that could last are our concepts, ideas. When nestled within a company, those concepts and ideas are the key to not only lasting decades but achieving impact.

If you can follow these prescriptive steps, you are going to use the one vessel that we have created as a species to enact change and enact change for good. Because we've tried with models. You're up against it.

Companies have been used in fairly exploitative fashions for several hundreds of years. But so have governments, so have monarchies. All different types of structures that we humans have conceptualized in our minds.

We've seen it even with nonprofits. What are they doing? Merely avoiding taxes. So it's not going to be that sector that helps us overcome our flaws either.

Don't you want to be an example? You can be the example of a company that not only succeeds, but thrives by truly doing good for the world.

The revenue model needs, first and foremost, a base of customers. So to put that first, you need to decide: am I going after a specific type of person? Can I get a proof of concept early? Can I make sure that that specific group of people is going to be willing and able to pay a premium amount of money for my product or service? That's the first thing I need to validate.

If I'm trying to serve a large body of people with a more affordable offering, the same principles still apply. You need to confirm early on if people are willing and able to spend that money.

Again, very simple tactics here are applicable. Can you serve a piece of messaging, an ad, and get appropriate signups? Get people to mock fill in credit card details. Those are good pieces of research to start with to just validate that, 'yes, my business model can succeed.'

The next step is opportunity identification. How do I start doing that? How do I find people that are different from the current market that I serve, but who may also have a similar problem?

They might look completely different, and you kind of want that. You want them to look completely different to your existing market of customers.

'Is there something in their needs that is exactly the same as mine? Can I then try my product or service offering with them? If I can, I'm building that opportunity. I'm building new streams.'

Once you're building those opportunities, they are not going to be confined to your current residence; whether it's a city, whether it's a country, or wherever you are physically located right now as a business owner, those opportunities may well be very far-flung. So you are quickly going to want to have experts in those regions.

And this still comes back to what we were saying about outsourcing versus insourcing. You don't have to have someone that is overseas, be full-time insourced, so you can try it out. That's the advantage of this business model. You can use outsourced talent to very quickly get an understanding of a particular market and do it in a fairly cost-effective manner.

Once you build those opportunities, look to that talent, look to bring that talent on quickly, even in a short-term engagement, so you can learn about those different markets very rapidly.

By building the resiliency that we mentioned and by building those opportunities, you're inevitably going to start to see a return. This is where you've got to put your financial hat on. You've got to look at it and think, 'am I building enough different revenue streams?' And then you now need to play them out.

'What if this one went down tomorrow? What if that one went down tomorrow?'

You need to start not banking on your current revenue streams for the future because this is the problem that happens time and time again. It's one of the biggest fallacies that humans do, thinking that what's happening now will continue into the future.

A classic example of this was the pandemic. A bunch of tech companies got huge valuations, definitely over-valuations, because they assumed that what was happening at that point in time was going to continue into the future. Then with the pandemic subsides, those valuations capitulated.

And so you're going to have to think against the grain on this one. You're going to have to think, 'hey, what if this business model evaporated tomorrow? What if this service is no longer relevant?'

Through that exercise, you will truly see how many different horses you've bet on. It's not just enough to say, hey, we've got three different markets. Are those three different markets serving the exact same type of person? If so, they're at risk.

You've realistically still got one horse. You need to look to see if there are enough differences between the different markets and the different products and services that you offer so that you truly have multiple horses, multiple lines of revenue, and, therefore, true diversification.

Don't start with impact in mind. When you start with impact in mind, you're going to speak in fairly ego-driven terms.

It's really hard; most humans do it.

You look at the humans who self-conceptualize "changing the world." They often appear too arrogant, too ego-driven. And why does this matter? It's not wrong to have a healthy ego, but you're operating from yourself.

If you're truly thinking about a business, you need to think about others. You need to obsess about others, because the only reason that your business will survive for decades is if you serve enough people with a problem that is critical enough for them to give you the funds to solve it.

If you don't conceptualize impact first and you actually just hone in on what others need, ironically enough, you will achieve global impact.

Chapter 6

Finding Success

You, Business Owner, have articulated a need, a need to grow a company for the long term. You're very apprehensive about going into this future world of massive uncertainty.

Perhaps you've been yearning for the days of the past, yearning for one of the most unique periods of history; that being from the 1990s through to 2005.

A lot of business owners in the contemporary world have grown up in that period. They've grown up with easy access to credit, relatively stable governments, relatively stable financial institutions, and, therefore, a relatively stable economic environment.

And you might think, 'hey, can we just get back to that time period? Can I just build my business the way that all successful businesses were built back in that time period?'

I'm here to tell you that not only is that a fallacy of your thinking, but that unique period from 1990 to 2005, just shy of the global recession, was a once-in-a-lifetime, once in a millennia phenomenon.

That ain't coming back.

The crisis that I am predicting is not a matter of something which 'might' happen, but it is a certainty that it will occur in some form.

We are never going to get back to those good times of stability and availability of easy resources for growth.

So you've got two options: You can continue to rail against reality and create a business based on those fallacies of the past. Or you can build agility and resiliency into your business model from the get-go.

I know which option I would prefer.

This is the only way to succeed going forward. There is going to be a lot of hurt. There's going to be a lot of pain for a lot of different companies as they continue to try and look to the past and try to make decisions based on it.

You can't do that.

Again, the financial industry has a saying that is very indicative, "past performance does not guarantee future results." Similarly, every data scientist worth their salt will tell you a very core fundamental truth: any form of data, no matter how large the body you collect, is meaningless when it comes to predicting the future.

So you might be asking, "well, why should I believe you, Patrick? If no one can predict the future, why can't I just blindly put my head in the sand and think things will be okay?" That is the exact point.

You are making your business decisions, currently, based on one set of circumstances. What I'm advocating for in this model is resiliency, agility, and the ability to not have a single point of failure. I am advocating for a business model that takes all situations and all circumstances into account. Not one that necessarily takes advantage of anyone.

You might not see stellar growth from one particular crisis with this model. You might not be used to having the economic opportunities you had in the past. But more importantly, you're not going to get a crisis that wipes you out.

That's why you should take advantage of this business model.

That's why you embrace it.

You embrace it not for the growth opportunities, but you embrace it to avoid complete annihilation.

I think here, we're talking about a perfect world. We're talking about an idea where a business owner is able to get exactly what they want out of their company. They're able to do it as efficiently as possible. They're able to do it economically, obviously. I'm not deluded. I know that if business owners are engaging, or even if they're receptive to something like outsourcing, they're thinking in terms of cost.

This particular chapter is pushing the idea that you're actually getting higher-quality talent. It's not just about getting cost benefits. It's also about getting quality benefits.

It still ties into a huge part of what was mentioned in the first couple of chapters, where it's not even about just getting success, but about building resiliency into your business model so you will achieve success regardless of the current crisis and possible disruptions.

That's really what we're trying to advocate here.

The Morgan Stanley CEO recently said that employees shouldn't have the right to choose where they work.

This was just the most idiotic statement I could have ever imagined. That's just short-term thinking. You're just trying to exercise some level of control. You're just trying to put all of your people into an in-person office for whatever reason.

And that rigid mindset is exactly what we're talking about here. Why are you trying to build single points of failure for your business?

You only have to look at climate change projections to know that half of Manhattan is going to be underwater in the next 50 years. Let's not try and create more inbuilt risks to our business models. There are going to be enough external risks over the next 50 to 100 years anyway without doing that.

We have a couple of core principles, and some of these are the same as what you've grown up with in learning business. But some of them are also radically different. The ones that are the same are the go-tos.

Are you solving a problem? Is that problem big enough and causing enough pain to enough people that they would be willing and able to pay for a solution? That's step number one.

Step number two, the customers. Your business model has to be agile, resilient, and adaptable over time. The only constant there is that your customers will change. Their needs, their problems, and things they want solved are going to change over time too.

You have to implicitly understand them. Not just in a superficial sense of name, age, and income level, but really down to the psychological level. What do they think about the world? Do they think about the world in the same way that you do? Do they not? They don't have to think the same way as you do, but you need to recognize those differences. Now that's pretty core. Customers.

The final one is operating structure. This is ensuring that you are always building up additional cash flows. Contingencies for those crises that I've mentioned.

That's the third step.

You always want to be making sure that you're not overleveraged, that you don't have too much debt. They always say compound interest is the eighth wonder of the world. You want compound interest working for you, not working against you.

Those three steps are the first batch. You might say, "pretty obvious, that's what I've been doing my entire life."

But now we need to look at the last two. These are where it becomes different, and most importantly, they are about inbuilt flexibility.

Do you have ongoing structures that you can't disrupt? These might be things like real estate terms.

Do you have a large office space? Do you have contracts with your employees that set them into a fixed way of thinking? Or are you able to provide them incentives so they can continue to learn, adapt, build new business models, experiment, and innovate? Are you actively creating a business that fosters that for your employees?

Are you able to create that so all of your employees can contribute to this company of yours that you've articulated, not just so it lasts for two years or five years, but so it is actually able to be successful for decades.

The final step is one that I've talked about many times before. Every business that is building itself in methods of the past is doing it in one single way, and that's creating single points of failure. You need to avoid this at all costs. You need to build ways of having contingencies.

This is right across the board. This is not having a single point of failure of location. Spread your team, get it global, get it distributed. Don't rely on one network infrastructure. Don't rely on one cloud vendor because, again, you don't know which crisis could take one of those out and your business along with it. Build multiple models. You don't know which revenue model will continue to succeed.

This is one of the biggest things that companies, even successful companies, still get plagued with to this day. They're too over-reliant on one set of revenue, and they make business decisions based on that. Realistically, their smaller startup competitors disrupt them. They can see the writing on the wall, but they don't know how to move the ship quickly enough.

Are you building multiple revenue models, multiple streams of income within your business? You might have, personally, multiple streams of income, but are you doing the same for your business? This is very critical. You need to avoid single points of failure.

There's going to be one theme that emerges in the next 50 to 100 years. It is that every single entity, person, nation, and institution failed because of the simple common reason that they had a single point of failure and were not able to adapt to changing circumstances.

Change is always constant, and I hear many of you always say it. You speak on stage when you give those keynotes; you're always saying change is constant.

How about you actually embrace it this time? How about you actually prove that you can live up to those words and build a business that is always ready to change?

Solving Problems

Solving problems should be nothing new to every business owner reading this book, because it is the core of business. Even if we go back to the fundamentals of monetary exchange. What is money? Money is a store of value.

We have collectively decided that rather than trade things. I give you some grain; you give me a goat. We have decided to use a financial intermediary, that is money. We all agreed that it consists of a certain value. That value might fluctuate, but it contains value.

When someone gives you money, in today's modern context, why are they doing it? They are doing it because you are making their life a little easier, a little more convenient.

Let's think about those two terms, 'easy' and 'convenient,' i.e., the flip side, you're alleviating pain. Therefore, that is everything you do in business. Every successful business that has ever been created has to solve a problem.

That problem can't just be a little problem. It can't be a mosquito buzzing in the air. It needs to be "my leg is bleeding and I need to bandage it." It needs to be a severe problem. A problem that will make people take action. A problem that will make people willing to part with that store of value that they have, i.e., money. That's nothing new for you.

Your challenge, when you're thinking about solving problems, is that you need to think in the long-term sense. You need to have short-term pain for your customers, because if they don't have that, your customers won't reach a threshold where they'll want to part with money in order to solve that problem.

At the same time, you need to recognize that these

problems will likely change. The problem that you solve with your business today may well be a different problem five years from now, 10 years from now, or 20 years from now.

That's the key here with problem-solving. You're going to do that your entire career, and you have, which is why you built successful businesses up until now.

However, you really need to realize that the scope and magnitude of those problems are going to change far more rapidly in the future than it ever has in the past.

The first step you will want to take: you always need to evaluate the scale and magnitude of the problem you're solving.

How do you do that? You go to customers, you research, and you need to figure out if the problem you're solving today is a 'nice to have' or a 'need to have.' What's the threshold of pain it's causing?

You need to be clever about this because even customers won't always give you the perfect answer. You can ask them questions like, "what would your world look like if my service or solution didn't exist? What does it mean to you? What does it allow you to accomplish? What is the best benefit of what my service or solution provides to you?"

Ask them, understand them. The irony is that their answers may well surprise you. What you think and why you think people give you money for what you do may well be very different to why they actually give you money. Make sure you survey them and remember that you always need to be living in the world of 'need to have.' You need to make sure that your business is constantly positioned towards critical problems.

If you're in the 'nice to have' category and you're exceedingly vulnerable, then you can only survive in good economic times with stable foundations and stable institutions. As we've already articulated, those times are going to be fewer and further between than ever before.

You can't position for the good times; you need to position for the bad. Ensure that you are a priority for your customers, and that they can't live without you.

Constants

The biggest mistake that business owners make when it comes to their customers is that they only learn about them through the lens of how they interact with their particular product, service, or solution.

That makes sense, because you might think, 'why do I need to understand every single thing about my customer? Why do I need that level of information?' You need that because it is a clear and very obvious truth of any sort of revenue generation function, that it is much easier to convince an existing customer than someone who has never spent any money on you.

You need to remember that every customer who has spent money on you has implicit trust and an implicit motivation, so give them that good favor that you have built. This is your number one priority.

A customer who doesn't feel fully understood by you will drop you as soon as your solution no longer meets their needs. You need to understand them more deeply than you could have possibly imagined if you want to avoid that happening. It's not enough to think about, 'how is this helping my customer achieve success in business?' You need to think about how it's helping them achieve financial and personal success in their relationships.

That's why you need to go really deep. That's why you need to look past the superficial thought of, 'how does my service or solution help you?' You need to go even deeper than simple demographics and psychographics.

There are a few tricks you can use here. You don't necessarily need to get every piece of information from the horse's mouth. It doesn't have to be an interrogation of your customers, but we do have various tools that allow you to infer.

You can base some information on personality types. You don't have to necessarily use one single one. I'm certainly not advocating for that. But you can use a combination. You can use a combination of Myers-Briggs, Enneagram, and DISC. Pull all of those together, and you'll start getting a better picture.

You have to record information correctly. Having a full picture of each of your customers in your CRM, making notes of how many children they have, where they live, what they care about, their hobbies, and are there any nonprofits they work for or donate their time to? Building up that body of data about your customer is critical.

Then you need to back up that gathering of information with some human empathy and care. Showing that you care for them throughout their lifetime. Even when they're perhaps not in a position to buy a particular product or service. Don't demonize them for that; embrace them.

Those happy customers will be your ticket to success and to surviving the crises. Those customers need to be understood. If you don't understand them, you're going to have to go out and convince more new customers. And why would you put yourself in that position? Especially when, with further crises on the horizon, it's only going to make people more apprehensive to buy. They're going to feel more unstable. And so, why would they take a chance on a new vendor?

Better for you to focus on the people you've already convinced and already built trust with and let them do the selling for you. Only then will your business continue to expand, thrive and survive.

This is where you need to build your army of resources. Business Owners, even if you want to care, you just don't have anything available to you. Too often, it's, "well, that's not my domain. I'm sorry. Best of luck."

But if you've done your job, if you've understood your customers implicitly, then you should know products and services and even advice don't necessarily have to be paid for. Maybe you have tips, tricks, hacks, or anything that you can provide; whether it's for free or whether it's paid doesn't matter.

It's about showing that you care about your customer more than just how they engage with your company financially. This should be very obvious, and it will take time to build this pool of resources. You should have a ready list of helpful advice for your customers if you've done your research correctly.

The quickest way to start with this, obviously, is the core thrust of your product or service and the core reason that your customers are buying.

There are likely some affiliated services that they also think about within the ecosystem of purchasing your product or service. So if that's the case, have ready recommendations for them. You don't need an extensive list. It doesn't need to be all fancy. It could even just be a simple spreadsheet. It can just be two to three recommendations across the board.

Start there, but don't just be complacent there. Continue to understand the evolving nature of that customer because your business is going to keep changing, and you, Business Owner, have to keep changing.

Once again, you can only count on one constant here. Your customers will change, so make sure that you are constantly adapting to their particular needs. They will follow you for decades to come if you're demonstrating that care.

Operating Structure

So when we move from our customers, because at the end of the day, if we're solving their problems and we're understanding them, then we're generating revenue, and that's great.

However, we have seen over the last three decades, let's call it, from the nineties through to now, business has been completely awash with credit, with capital. Business owners like yourself, some of them have been mindful of their operating structure, but many have thrown caution to the wind in order to take advantage of this environment.

It's problematic because it means taking on too much debt. It's problematic because it means hiring more people than you need. It's problematic because it means splashing the cash on a fancy office in the middle of a major metropolitan city just because that's the done thing to do.

If you've been mindful about how you generate your revenue and what revenue you can generate, then you equally need to be mindful of your cost. That comes through your operating structure. You need to build that flexibility. You need to avoid those long-term liabilities.

It's important to draw the distinction between liabilities that produce a return for you versus sunk-cost liabilities. What do we think of when we think of sunk-cost liabilities? We think of underutilized real estate. We think of office space that is just sitting there. We think of utilities that have to be used for that office space.

Electricity, water, gas. Those fixed liabilities are sunk-costs. Do they benefit your business? Maybe in a temporary sense, but not in a long-term sense. Not in a sense of building resiliency and agility into this model.

We need to also compare that, however, to the operating cost of your people. Every business owner likes to talk about how valuable their people are. Yet in this same breath, they talk about how people, i.e., salaries, are their biggest cost and biggest expense. This is not to say that you need to cut employees when times get tough. On the contrary, those are the liabilities that will generate returns for you. Those are the people that, when you invest in them, can help you navigate the turmoils of the market, because it can't just be down to you.

You are one perspective, a very bright perspective, but one perspective nonetheless. In order for your company to continue to survive, you need multiple different perspectives at all times to meet the unique demands of whatever the next crisis may bring.

However, you can still look at your operating structure to make sure you are being efficient, make sure you're not over-leveraged, and make sure you're not taking on too much debt. While growth is important here, it's not the singular goal.

That has been the problem for the last three decades. That growth, at all costs, has been the mantra. It has been an easy mantra to follow when the markets have been awash with free, or next to free, access to capital. It made it very easy to get financial investment.

That's not happening in the long-term.

What do you have to do if you can't depend on those financial institutions for easy access to capital and credit? What do you do tomorrow? What you do tomorrow is, again, go back to the simple income statement. Go back to your operating costs. What is fixed? What is not? Where can you find efficiencies within what your cost is right now? When you can find those efficiencies, then you can really start to look at how agile your business truly is.

One of the biggest areas here is cash flow. You might think, 'well, hey, I've got a cash reserve because I am able to pay for my taxes.' It's a fairly common use for many businesses.

We need to think beyond that. We need to think beyond merely paying taxes year to year.

You might think in terms of cash flow for investment. Perhaps you don't want to take on outside funding, and you'd be smart to not want to do that because you might end up overleveraged with debt you can't service if you do.

There are many prolific public examples. The most recent one with Twitter comes to mind, where a company is put into debt and put in a very difficult situation to service that debt. You don't want to do that, but you also want to think even more expansively than that. You want to critically look at that cash reserve because cash money is the lifeblood of any business.

This shouldn't be news to you, but it's going to be increasingly important, especially when other areas of financing that you are used to are no longer viable. Easy access to credit? Gone in the future.

When a crisis happens, and you're relying on the government to bail you out, what happens if the government's defaulting? It's gone.

Every institution that you have been traditionally raised to believe is rock solid is actually very shaky. It only takes a handful of crises back to back before all the cards come crumbling down.

This is not to say that's a negative. You don't need that to happen to you. If you're generating revenue, that's wonderful. That can go in an instant.

The only way you can survive is by making sure your operating structure is efficient, economical and doesn't overleverage yourself.

Inbuilt Flexibilities

If you built your business to generate revenue and have an efficient cost structure, that's table stakes. You understand that better than anyone. You, as a business owner, spend most of the time obsessed about the finances. Even the most financially illiterate business owners will spend the majority of their time thinking about the finances, because it is literally do or die.

However, we need to bring in a new dimension. Inbuilt flexibility. We've been building businesses based on revenue generation and cost structure for a world that is rapidly diminishing in how it exists. A frame of reference that no longer exists. We need to think of new ways.

This is where your true shining innovation will come.

It is not going to be in the world of technology, though that world will continue to get the headlines. The true innovation that will allow you to survive will be you building a flexible business model that survives any shock in the system. And you can stop now. We still have some blueprints. You don't have to do this all on your own. It's not just going to be on you to come up with all the ideas.

We have models tied to employee ownership. You can share that ownership with your employees to make them equally invested.

We also have, on the flip side, real estate, co-working spaces, month to month contracts. You don't have to lock yourself into a particular city or a particular space. Building that flexibility is good.

You can build incentive programs for your employees, incentive programs that accrue benefits to them over the long term so they have a reason to be interested and invested in your company. You can also build them programs in a way that incentivizes experimentation and innovation. You're going to have to build a model for that because most employees will look out for their own heads.

It's just natural human nature. We don't like to stick our neck out on the line.

If that is the default, you now need to look at those employment contracts and think, 'how can I overcome that? How can I incentivize behavior over and above what people would do? Can I show them and demonstrate to them that they're not going to be punished when they take the risk and experiment?' Those are some of the early ways you can think about it, but you need to think more holistically.

You need to think about the crises of the future. This is where you can play them out with existing business resiliency experts. 'What are the crises that could happen? How would that affect my business? Would my business be able to adapt?'

You don't necessarily have to have the experience happen to you to be able to plan for it. 'What happens if a war happens in a particular region where some of my employees are? Are there enough other employees in other parts of the world that could be safe, that could continue the function of the business?'

If a particular country is in economic turmoil, what does that mean for your business? Does that change how much your customers can give you money? Are you able to continue to survive because you have enough cash flow?

These are the questions you need to be asking yourself. Not just about, 'am I building a flexible business for today?' But, 'am I building a flexible business to survive?'

Conversely, thinking about it within the dimension of crisis doesn't need to be pessimistic. The irony here is, by doing this exercise and continuing to evaluate this exercise through the lens of flexibility, you are also going to avail yourself of opportunity.

You don't have to focus on just one body of customers to service and you can service customers from right across the world if you're not tied to a location. If you have employees in markets right across the world, they can see opportunities before they become public knowledge and seize on them early. They'll see new innovations, new ways of doing things earlier than you might otherwise. That is the advantage of flexibility.

While you do need to think about it in terms of business survival, and that's incumbent on you as a leader, you will then want to ensure that there is flexibility in the business model so it could survive for five years, for 10 years, for 20, for 50.

You will want to make sure of that, but you're also going to get opportunities. And you're also going to grow through those opportunities. You're also going to thrive.

Contingencies

Why do you need contingencies? Because your business will take a hit. Every business will. Every person will. And every nation will.

We have just come off the back of one of the greatest periods of peace that the world has ever known. Unfortunately, it's been fleeting. It's been temporary. No one is ready for the reckoning that will come. No one can even predict which particular reckoning it will be.

Will it be a climate crisis? Will it be war? Will it be resource depletion? It could be a combination of all three.

How will that affect institutions? How will that affect communities? How will that knock onto markets? Only time will tell.

But what isn't up for debate is that disruptions are coming, and they will impact you. Your only key to surviving is having multiple escape pods. Those escape pods are the contingencies, so you're not beholden to one market. You're not beholden to one location. You're not beholden to one set of ideas, one set of values.

You are able to succeed by creating a truly globally-minded, distributed company. With that, you are able to thrive no matter what happens. If you've followed these steps up until now, you've got a lot of those contingencies already built out.

You just, once again, need to apply your mind to thinking, 'if this function of my business went away tomorrow, could I still survive?' You need to think right across the board. You need to think of the inanimate parts of your business. i.e., 'If this region, this country, this office space, if that went away tomorrow, would my business still survive?'

You also need to think of the human side. 'What if there's turmoil in this region of the world where a large body of my employees are? What would that mean for my business?'

When you build in these contingencies, it's not that disruption won't happen. It obviously will. But your business will not diminish entirely because you'll have contingencies ready. We've seen some businesses survive this way.

Some businesses, even to this day, have a heritage that has lasted 100 years, some 150. Not many have lasted more than that. They've gone through different iterations. They've seen lots of financial crises. Hats off to them.

You've got to be even better than that. You've always been up for a challenge. It's why you got into business. This is going to be the most monumental challenge of your life because you're not just going to deal with one dimension.

You're not just going to have to deal with the fluctuations of a capitalist free market economy and the boom and busts of a financial cycle. That's one dimension of the future. You're going to deal with demographic change in the same breath. How do you manage when most of the productive workforce is into their retirement?

You're going to have to deal with resources being at an all-time low and being even more costly than we've gotten used to throughout the industrial age. You're going to deal with political and social instability as people grapple with a new world order where things are more expensive.

Perhaps the world becomes more fearful. You don't have to let your business suffer for that reason.

You can create contingencies so your business will always thrive. You will want to do this, not just selfishly for your own reason (although that's as good a motive as any), but because you will be an example for the world. You will show the world that there is a path forward despite all of this chaos and uncertainty.

Humans have been incredibly resilient and adaptable creatures their entire existence. If you can be that one small example, if one business can meet the challenges of tomorrow, then why can't every business?

That's why you build contingencies, because you will build an example, a long-lasting business, and ultimately a legacy that will live on through the ages.

You might think that rigidly and unforgivingly controlling all dimensions of your business is the correct path to take. You may think that you are giving your businesses a chance to survive by doing that.

I am here to tell you that you are categorically wrong. You are wrong because you are acting like you can control everything. That is one of the simplest tenets of all of us as humans.

We can control, let's call it 10% of what's in our purview. The other 90%, we can't. So why would we pretend? If there's anything we learned from the crises of the past, we can look at pandemics, we can look at wars, we can look at economic crises. No one person can stop them.

Applying a rigid and unforgiving mindset to your company is destined to fail. You're only going to survive a handful of years until the next crisis disrupts you.

So why would you do that? Why would you build a business that is inherently guaranteed to fail? You don't know when, but it will.

Instead, wouldn't you rather build a business that can actually succeed? Wouldn't you rather build a business that has flexibility, that has care for the world, that has care for its employees, that has care for its customers? Wouldn't you rather build a business that is operating in sync with nature, not only with human nature but the wider environment?

If there's anything we've learned, it's that the more humans grip tighter to try and control the entity that they are trying to control, whether it's an employee, an institution, or a market, the quicker it slips out of our grasp.

You cannot control the future. We cannot predict the future. But we do know an acceleration is happening.

We do know that we are going to continue to face more turmoil.

It's not going to get any easier.

We've had it. We've had the easiest run in multiple millennia. We've never had it this easy. Think of the industries that exist that weren't even imaginable in the past. Think of the population that we have on this planet that we've never had before and how quickly that came about.

If it can only get harder, we can respond in one of two ways. We can respond with fear, or we can respond with abundance. If we respond with fear when we try to control, we are inevitably going to lose control. And it will cause pain and suffering.

But if we focus on abundance, on resilience, on agility, then we could create not only businesses that the world needs but also the systems, institutions, people, societies, and ultimately, the world that we would like to live in.

Chapter 7

A Better Future

When you do it well, thinking about 'how and when you should look after people' – while it might seem tough – will benefit your business time and time again.

Everything we've talked about up till now is sort of akin to prescribing the steps, but I would like this chapter to perhaps take a more macro view.

The business owner that's reading this is likely to spend the majority of their time on the steps required because it's what they can do today and it's the learning they can put into practice right now.

I think what still needs to be said, the thrust of what I'm hoping to get across with this chapter, is that the space of outsourcing has had such a dirty connotation for the entirety of its history. It always gets put in colonialistic terms or in terms of exploitation, and what I think gets missed is that, yes, if used incorrectly, it can be that way. But realistically, when you look at the best success stories, outsourcing is about people getting to do what they do best.

It's people getting paid more to do what they do best. And ultimately, at its simplest level, it's a 'the tide raises all boats' philosophy. And that, I think, is really where we should be headed.

Let's go back to when "outsourcing" started.

For the longest time in human history, outsourcing was essentially impossible. You can literally go all the way back to "where did we start?" We started as little river people that congregated around bodies of water because those were the easiest places to grow food.

We started from that, and we expanded into larger and larger places, city metropolises where everything was essentially in service of agriculture.

To fast forward, we went through a period of intense conflict as weapons became more sophisticated into what we would call the modern era through the Renaissance. And finally, once we're truly getting to what we would start to recognize as the world today, we went into the colonial era. This was the 1800s. This was the first time that nations were really developing products and services to be sold en masse.

Again, that has a checkered past. You basically had European powers scrambling for more and more of the world. They took markets, they took the resources of those markets, turned them into finished goods, and sold them to the wealthy upper classes of their own nations.

Fast forward once again to, realistically, specific outsourcing, i.e., tech outsourcing, which is the thrust of what I'm good at. But even there, we only have a few key innovations.

We have transportation innovations that allow vast distances to be traveled quickly, and we have telecommunications innovations that allow people to be connected right around the world. Only at this point do you start to get the ability to truly have different countries specialized. Realistically, we're looking at post-World War II when this happens.

But even when that happens, and the world starts to lean into specializing in different areas, this still has this flavor of colonialistic exploitation that is embedded inherently from the get-go.

Why is that? Well, the first big wave of tech outsourcing,

right or wrong, unfortunately, came within the 1980s. The 1980s were very famous for two big people– Reagan and Thatcher–and very famous for neoliberal policies right across the board in terms of political structure and in terms of economics.

We can debate the merits of their policies, and we can debate whether they were particularly good people; I would argue most certainly not. They did, in many cases, irreparable damage to working classes in both the US and the UK without much care. You also had it coinciding with something that was happening in the private sector, a detachment from what was previously stakeholder capitalism, shareholder capitalism.

This is actually the world that still exists to this day. There was actually a time when companies didn't do mass layoffs and did care about how they contributed to their community and didn't just try and dodge taxes.

So it's not that outsourcing itself is evil or good by its very nature; it's neutral. It's just a function.

If the function is used correctly, it can be really supportive of the wider world's ability to heal itself, but it has been baked, molded, and created in a context that has allowed people to tarnish it and develop their own theme of what outsourcing is.

You may have heard people analyzing why outsourcing is even a case. People will say it was that companies had the first opportunity to take labor and put it offshore, and they did. They slashed costs, the experience was worse, corporate profits ballooned, and the common man was left behind.

Make no mistake, that all happened, but that shouldn't be the only way that outsourcing is viewed because, in the same breath, didn't you see, and now we bring it all the way up to the current day, what happened during the pandemic?

We had supply chain issues, and while there is a more functional form of outsourcing, you started to see the media pieces that celebrated a return to American manufacturing.

Reshoring is literally the concept of bringing jobs back from overseas to your country, and even in that, there is something aggressively nationalistic about it. It is, in many ways, also colonialistic, because you're assuming, 'oh, we're done with cost cutting via work done by foreigners and we're bringing it back to good old red, white and blue American values.'

I would like to propose a third way. You don't have to view all of the outsourcing through the lens of overseas just being about cost and numbers, because they're people too. You don't have to view it as reshoring to America being the only other option. It's a more expensive option, but it's a better option and it's a more secure option.

What I would argue is, if we're actually serious about

realizing the promise of a truly global economy, then surely we should be able to engage in outsourcing in a way that isn't exploitative.

It's going to take time, it's going to involve cost saving, and I'm not naive to that future. But if outsourcing continues to succeed and different groups of people start to raise their incomes, then suddenly, the cost basis starts to go away.

The business owner might ask, "well, isn't that the whole reason I'm doing this? Why would I deal with people who are overseas if I'm not making savings?"

Let's talk about that horizon because that, I think, is a fallacy. We've got two main areas to look at.

The first is technology. Technology continues to condense and compress the differences between us as humans, even down to a fundamental of real-time translation technology. It has made it easier and easier to speak with people from different cultures and from different backgrounds without even having to mandate that English is the only language they know.

That, combined with the fact that English rates continue to skyrocket as people from all across the world realize that learning English is economically beneficial, means that we can foresee a time in the future where we essentially are all speaking the same language. So that's one side of it.

Secondly, it comes back to that promise of specialization, in that there are people and cultures who start to lean into what they do best, and by trading with one another, they once again realize the economic benefit of free trade.

We can get into all the arguments of whether that creates a disadvantage for others, but the economics of it is very sound. You will always create more net value for the entire globe by doing it in that way.

Isn't it about time we actually realized that promise rather than continuing to hold to these old ideals of nationalism like, "yeah, but I'm still going to do it here in this city or this state or this country because that's my home and that's a safer way of doing it."

Wouldn't you rather tap into the very best functions right across your entire company? I think that really is what it boils down to.

Yes, if you do outsourcing today, do you get a cost saving? Of course you do.

Even when you can't get that cost saving in the future, I would argue you would still do outsourcing because, by doing it, you're able to tap into the absolute brightest minds across the world for all the different types of functions that your business needs.

If you can do that, that's the only way you're going to cre-ate a resilient and agile business that survives through any sort of turmoil. Not only will it survive any sort of turmoil, but it will actually act as an example for how we can have truly sustainable outsourcing models around the world.

Hopefully, if this continues to happen in a way that's mutually beneficial, both for the business owners who do the outsourcing as well as the individuals who are performing the work in an outsourcing way, then perhaps we can detach it from history.

This is one of the biggest challenges facing humans. We find it really hard to analyze the past because the past is tainted. The past is tainted by the perspectives of those who wrote it. This is another form of the classic adage, 'history is written by victors.' But the funny thing is, we now see an alternative.

We don't just face the challenge of the victors writing the past, but then other people come in with their own lens and rewrite the past again.

Then someone comes in again and rewrites it again, and through this, you get this amorphous of narratives rather than the truth. We see this all the time. We see that certain viewpoints have been recorded by a certain construct of a particular civilization of the past. We then find out some more information, and it turns out it was completely different, and then we view it through certain "-isms," or lenses if you will. That doesn't work either.

Through all that, we always need to remember that humans are very quick to create narratives. Humans are really sold by narratives very effectively. It's a lot harder to battle against these negative perceptions of outsourcing purely because of the narrative around it and the time period around it is viewed so negatively.

Especially right now, because we can't escape our current context, we're in a context where we're seeing economic turmoil increasing in how rapidly it happens. Because of that, we're looking for causes, and rightly or wrongly, the current flavor of the day is to blame the neoliberalism of the 1980s.

Now that may or may not be the cause of our current suffering, but it doesn't do well to blame all things that happened during that time period as a consequence.

There is a world where outsourcing is contributing a net positive to this planet.

Better Business Models

When we look at company business models and how companies have played since shareholder capitalism has taken root, we, unfortunately, look at what is known as double-entry accounting. Double-entry accounting is a simple way that every business measures their profit and loss. It's a standard income statement. You have assets on one side, and you have liabilities and debt on the other.

The biggest problem with this model, while it has seen enormous growth and companies succeeding right across the board with it, is that it has led to this reductionist type of business that only looks at people in terms of being a number. On top of that, it looks at everything in terms of numbers.

It looks at equipment, it looks at talent, it looks at every component of a business purely by what can be measured in terms of its economic value or economic utility to the business. While that is important because cash is obviously needed for businesses to survive, and I'm not under any illusions about that, it continues to foster short-term thinking. It continues to foster thinking that is purely focused on 'how can I make more money this quarter, this year. How can I take advantage of this opportunity? How can I do more with less?'

All of these phrases and all of these terms are essentially not thinking about the broader picture of where a business operates. It's purely thinking in extractive terms, like, 'how much less can I pay my employees? How much more can I charge my customers? How much cheaper can I get the equipment or the resources? How much less can I pay on my taxes?'

All of these concepts, however nobly you want to doll them up, ultimately come down to extraction, and extraction is just another word for exploitation. That just isn't going to work. It can't work in the future. We need to move towards replenishment, and I think this concept of replenishment can happen right across the board.

Can you charge your customers an appropriate amount of money for the value you're providing? Can you pay your employees an appropriate amount of money that allows them to thrive and succeed? Can you not take so many resources out of the planet and actually contribute a net positive to a sustainable future?

These are the business models that you need to focus on, because the funny thing here is that it's not anything new. It's stakeholder capitalism, but on steroids. You just have to take what we've already learned.

Companies can go back to this, but they'll go back to it in a different way. Rather than the stakeholder capitalism that existed in the 1940s, and 1950s America, where they focused on how they were contributing to their local communities, this time around, they'll focus on how they're contributing to the global community. That is the key here.

It's about doing those little things right across the board. Because now that you have access to the globe, you can create a business model that isn't extractive. You can be mindful of what your net impact on the world is, both in terms of what resources you're using and how you're treating your staff and your customers.

Better Economies

There is always this strong tendency for an economy to be conflated with a nation. When you conflate it with a nation, you start getting into superiority complexes about particular nations.

This goes all the way back, funnily enough, to the origins of branding and marketing. The origins of that go back to the French in the 1700s. They did not realize that the world didn't want what they were offering, so they made it fashionable. They made it high class. They made it synonymous so that if you wanted the best quality fashion or the best quality food, it had to be French food.

This is one of those toxic values that has persisted in almost every nation and needs to die. There is this simplistic, almost tribal, Neanderthal way of thinking, that if something comes from a certain nation, it is good, and if something comes from a different nation, it is bad. People will gloss it up. They'll say, "oh, I'm just looking out for the individual," or, "I'm looking out for my city." Isn't it about time that we, as a species, especially facing the existential crises that we are, started thinking as one species rather than along the lines of these manufactured divisions between ourselves?

The fact of the matter is, we share 100% of our DNA with one another. We're really not that different from each other right across the world. Yes, you can argue, "but what about culture, Patrick?" Fuck that. It's superficial; it really is. At our core essence, we are the same, and if we are the same, we need to really detach this idea that an economy is purely related to a nation. Because when we're building better economies, everyone wins.

We need to create systems where we are being contributive to one another and not extractive. When you purely think in extractive terms, it is finite. You cannot, by definition, create economies based on extraction because, eventually, it runs out. We see this already with developed nations who have taken most of the resources for themselves, and developing nations then don't have much left for themselves.

So how do you counteract that? By creating a contributive world. If every economy is contributing to the betterment of the planet, then you're no longer playing in finite terms; you're playing in infinite terms. This is not just being contributive in the physical sense, but you can do it right across the board, both from a physical, mental, and emotional point of view, and meet all of the needs that humans have.

If you create those economies to be not the zero-sum game of the past, where it's, "if my economy is winning, your economy is losing," then suddenly you're creating a world where there is more wealth to go around and more wealth to support people of all social classes, cultures, and backgrounds. That's ultimately what we need to move towards because economic systems and most of the economic theories, unfortunately, were born in an era of extraction. They were born during an era of colonialism.

Even some of the great writers, like Adam Smith, pushed back against this idea. They realized that extraction couldn't be used in the way it was. Unfortunately, their messages get co-opted, they get twisted around, and they get turned into something they're not to support people's extractive short-term desires.

But if we truly look at what the greatest economic writers of history were advocating for, we can see the blueprint. We can see the blueprint based on a free and open exchange of goods and services and having communication right across the countries between people of all backgrounds and allowing the true benefit of specialization to happen. Once people specialize independently of their nation, that's when we start seeing the true explosions of growth that you can have, and that makes these economies turn for the better.

The key here to why we need a one-species economy is because it all comes back to the money multiplier effect. When you keep money and value stored away, when you don't put it into the economies, you get a multiplier effect in both senses. So when people are extracting and purely focused on how much they can hoard, they inevitably do not spend that money. When that money gets spent, it cascades throughout multiple areas of that economy, raising the overall level of wealth. When we look at why you will want to be a one-species economy, and indeed why you will want to be a business owner who is advocating for this and showing the way with your own business model, it's that you are actually going to be enhancing the wealth of the globe. By doing that, you yourself are going to be richer because, suddenly, you've got that money multiplier effect working in your favor.

Suddenly, with more people making more money, they have more money to spend on goods and services right across the board that can support even more businesses. It also supports your business because everyone isn't having to pinch pennies, and therefore looking at your offering thinking, "I can't can't spend on that. It's too expensive."

This is the key. You really want to be pushing for a unified economy because as soon as we go into our shell, as soon as we go back towards nation-based tendencies, or even all the way down to the local level, just protecting your patch of land, inevitably, we end up in a world of scarcity and decline. Ever-shrinking profits, ever-shrinking revenue, ever-shrinking opportunity. You have to flip that on its head.

You have to focus on abundance. And it's not just about focusing on abundance for abundance's sake, but if more people are prospering, if you are showing the way with your business that operates right across the globe, then suddenly the world is getting richer and as the world gets richer, you get richer.

Better Innovation

One of the things that continues to hold back humanity is lost institutional knowledge and a lack of expertise to drive change forward. What do I mean by that? When you focus on a national level, you have different countries learning at different rates. Some countries are able to make huge advances forward, whilst some are still learning lessons that others have learned many decades prior.

When we really look at the world of innovation, what does it come down to? It comes down to two key things. It comes down to, first and foremost, being able to absorb the majority of knowledge, and then it comes down to understanding all of that prior knowledge and thinking of a better way. Now, how do you get that to happen?

Well, we have the first tool, the tool to absorb all knowledge, which sits right here in our pockets. The cellphone.

We haven't used it as well as we should have for the last several decades, but it's there, and if it's a tool that we could use properly, that's fine. More importantly, we need to stop going back to square one, because this stop-start motion that countries keep having happens when someone advances a field, but then we forget that knowledge. We're very quick to lose the lessons of the past. Instead, we need to tap into the foremost experts around the world, because if we're truly creating companies that embrace A-class talent. That's when we're going to unlock innovation.

So what do I mean by this? To unlock A-class talent, you need to look right across the different functions of your business. Consciously or subconsciously, you have been focused on a particular function within your business. Maybe, by definition of holding it to a certain region or a certain location, maybe you've only got C-class talent.

Maybe you physically cannot get the best of the best. If you expand your scope to the world, you will be able to get A-class talent for every single function of your business. When you're able to do that, the magic happens. That is how innovation happens.

That is the world that we need to be in because right now, what happens? We have stratified levels of talent. We even see this on the recruiting side; candidates are ranked from A to B to C to D. The irony of that is a lot of that talent shouldn't even be in those fields. If we truly created globalized business models or globalized economies, then each person would have the space and the room to do exactly what is most authentic to them.

By doing that, they would be able to have the ability to deliver their A-level of talent in a function that is uniquely related to their skill set. That's the key to innovation because I think one of the key things here is that people think that there is some finite amount of A-class talent and that it is always a mad scramble for that. I would argue something different.

I would say that every single person on this planet has a core set of expertise, and that expertise is born based on what they know and what they've experienced. Because every individual has that unique experience, they have a slightly unique way of viewing both the industry, the work they've done, and the world in general.

If we can start tapping into that, we can unlock true innovation. What is innovation? Innovation, at its heart, is looking at the status quo of a product, of the good of service, of a business, of an economy, of a piece of technology, and saying, "the status quo is not good enough. We need something better." That's innovation.

To get that, you have to rely on the one thing that we've relied on since the entire formation of our species. The one thing that we have that no other species does. A conscious brain. That conscious brain has enormous, enormous potential. Potential that, I would argue, we still haven't fully unlocked.

If we could allow each person to do what is uniquely suited to them, wouldn't we create waves of innovation unprecedented in human history? That might seem like a big concept, and it is, but you can at least start today. You can start today by dispensing with your old-held values, those assumptions that one country is better than the other, that domestic is better than outsourced.

Instead, look at it objectively. For each of the functions that you have in your business, where is the best possible place to recruit? Who is the best possible person to support the innovation goals that every company needs? With innovation comes opportunity.

Better Talent Outcomes

Obviously, better businesses, better economies, and better innovation are all benefits that directly accrue to the business owner. If you're really looking at creating a business that we've talked about, one that is contributive and one that is a net positive for the world, then we still need to look at something that isn't necessarily a direct benefit. It can be over the longer term, but it doesn't come directly, as you might expect, and that's looking after your talent.

You're fighting a hard battle here because a lot of companies have tended towards extractive methodologies, and they've tended towards positioning their workers against capital. This is a story as old as time, and as long as the industrial revolution has existed, there's been a fight between capital and machinery and labor. That, once again, is a zero-sum game.

When you look at how you are treating your employees, you really need to come to the core of what it means to be human, to show empathy and compassion, to allow people to do their best possible work, to allow them to truly flourish, to reach their next potential. The fact of the matter is, so many of the businesses that sit around you may indeed have inspired you to go into business, but they have been built on faulty assumptions of how to treat workers. They've been built to treat workers with suspicion. They've been built to treat workers as nothing more than overgrown children, and ultimately, they've been built to treat workers with distrust.

The fact of the matter is, all humans are searching for meaning. They do this throughout their entire lives, and that is not going to change. That's wired into our DNA. Every single person, the moment they're born, the moment they start grabbing consciousness, their first instinct is to ask why. Why am I here? Why does it matter?

If that is the existential foundation of humanity, then isn't it incumbent on you to create a business and a world in which that person's existential thought can be realized?

And you might say, "that's not my job." Oh, on the contrary, it is exactly your job. The reason it's your job is because when you take care of your talent to that level, you're not just taking care of them financially. You're not just taking care of them emotionally. You're not just taking care of them physically, but really, you're taking care of them spiritually.

When you're taking care of them to that level, you allow them the space, and indeed, the ability, to truly realize their potential, and if you're the cause of that potential being realized, then this, once again, comes back to the benefits that you accrue.

It might be long-term. It might not be as direct as you believe, but that talent that you have invested in, that talent will pay dividends to you over the life of your business. Suddenly, their creative ideas come to you first. Their new business models, their new innovations, they come to you first. Their way of doing things comes to your business and your business alone because you've shown them that you can invest in their prosperity for the long term, and so they will invest in yours.

Better World

The example that I always default to here is the virtual assistant industry, because the virtual assistant industry is one of the most exploitative and extractive industries on the entire planet. It has been molded based on the economic exploitation of individuals.

Look at the regions that it happens most in—the Philippines and India—why does it happen in those regions? It happens in those regions because there isn't as much economic opportunity within those nations, and so the people are forced to look outside of themselves. Because there is not much economic opportunity, people and other companies, being aware of it, feel they can take advantage of it.

A classic example of this was Delta Airlines. They put their call center in the Philippines, and it was reportedly unspeakable how toxically they treated those call center workers. Why did that happen? Because they were just viewed as numbers. They were just viewed as, 'oh, it doesn't matter if we treat them really poorly with poor wages, someone else will come in and replace them.'

Compare that to a model that I have personally experienced. I look at the virtual assistants that have worked for me over the years, both across India and the Philippines. With those same places that other companies and other countries have chosen to extract from, I chose a different way. I chose to look at them not as numbers, but how they can contribute to my overall effort.

What did I do? For starters, I paid them more. Three times more. Three times more than the going rate. What did that do? You would argue that's insane.

Why did I create a higher cost basis? Because of what it yielded. That yielded stories like, "hey, I learned Python in my off time so that I can be more productive." An assistant literally learned an entire coding language; they didn't just do a task. And yet, we look at the industry of virtual assistants at large, and most of them just do what they're told.

I took an industry that was known to be full of order-takers, and I turned someone into a strategist because I cared for them at their core level. Putting that talent first, like I said before, pays dividends; it comes up with innovation and new ways of doing things. When you do that, suddenly there, I see a model for the world, for the future.

It's a small example, but imagine if we applied that same thinking, that same methodology right across the board with people of every function, of every background. Those are the small steps we could take. We could apply this same methodology and get some enormous wins very quickly in so many different industries simply by going in and observing the extractive history and the extractive nature of different functions and instead turning it into being contributory.

Now, it is a gamble, you are having to place a lot of faith in people, but as I said before, us humans are not that different. If you demonstrate that you care and if you give people the space and the psychological safety to be creative and innovative, they will be.

To go back to those virtual assistants, they have not left me in four years. Yet, the industry has an enormous turnover. Why? Because everyone views them as extractive, so they are extractive in turn. They leave for 50 cents more an hour, a dollar more an hour. Because it's all in financial terms. When you show that you care, you do not lose that talent. You do not lose that knowledge. You do not lose that innovation. Because they then stay loyal to you, and then you get the really wonderful stories.

It's all well and good to say, "hey, I managed to increase the productivity of my company's virtual assistants by 30%, 40%, 50%." That's all well and good, but it's when you've made a true impact in their lives that it really hits home.

It's stories like, "my wife went into labor and we were worried about the costs associated but with the extra money we now have, I was able to put her into the very best hospital." That matters.

We all talk in the world of economies about raising living standards, and of course, that's what we all want. We want to have a better future for ourselves than our parents did. We want our kids to have a better future than we do, but nothing makes it more tangible than the demonstrable difference that you can create in a person's life if you avoid being extractive and think more in terms of 'how can I contribute, how can I serve?'

This industry of virtual assistants is only one industry, yet, what if we applied this thinking to salespeople, engineers, designers, marketers, product strategists, manufacturers, real estate, finance, and insurance? What if we did it with business models right across the world? To ultimately create not just a fairer world, not just a more moral world, but a wealthier world, a more prosperous world, and ultimately a world we can be proud of.

You are fighting the toughest battle of your life, because if you think starting a business is tough, try changing human perception. Not just the human perception of the now, that's easy, but literally the human perception of generations and of history. It is a lofty goal to not want to hurtle towards destruction. But that's where we are; we're living in the world of extraction, and if no one does anything, we will continue on the path of least resistance.

This all comes back to the laws of motion. The absence of any other force, something that will continue to move in the path that it already was in, is called inertia. The problem is that our world's on a path of inertia that is not productive for it, that is not healthy for it.

If you are serious about creating a business that is globalized in nature, that cares for its employees, that is able to tap into the talent right around the world, that is able to get away from these colonialistic vestiges of the past and chart a new course through outsourcing, you will be able to create businesses that will knock on to economies, that will knock on to the world, that truly improves not only your life but others' lives too as well as the planet you live on. That's what it's all about. The planet, our home.

This isn't about deluding ourselves into thinking we'll just take those same colonialistic tendencies and apply them to other planets. That's just not learning from history. Wouldn't it be better for us to get it right here first?

Yes, you're up against it. You're trying to change the world, and not just the world physically, but the world mentally. You're trying to show a path forward for how the world can truly operate on a long-term replenishment horizon and not one of short-term extraction.

It is going to take a lot of work, and you won't be able to do it alone. But what you can do is be an example. Humans are very good at building momentum, and we're very good at getting into a herd mentality. Why are we in an extractive world? Other people are in an extractive mindset, so then we feel that we have to default to an extractive mindset. Otherwise, we won't get ahead. And it goes on and on and on.

Humans know, at their core, when they're doing something good for the world and when they're doing something poor for it, so they just need ideas.

They just need a concept. You can be that.

Your business can be that.

And if you can be that light on the hill, let the herd, let the momentum, let the rest of humanity come to your way of being.

But it is going to take you to take that first step and to build that business that can be the light.

Not just a light on the hill but also a light for the world.

Conclusion

In science fiction, the threat has always been portrayed as something external, like alien innovation. But the real threat is internal, and it's already among us. In the depths of my experience, I know we need the best and the brightest minds right across the world and the whole of humanity coalescing against the greatest threat to our survival.

I am putting a huge stake in the ground for the outsourcing world, distributed companies, and global collaboration, not because I think it will solve all problems but as a framework for us to debate, discuss and ultimately build resilience in the face of present and future challenges. For more people to see that is a way to foster deeper connections by reinforcing us back to the idea of stewardship.

I take pride in my career of taking on really boring industries that people, more often than not, neglect and don't
appreciate how much it impacts their lives. Despite its
mundane reputation, outsourcing has a significant impact
on individuals worldwide, whether you like it or not. And
there's the rub.

For instance, in the United States, some people accuse outsourcing of stealing jobs, even though it hasn't. Automation
has actually eliminated far more jobs than outsourcing. In
other parts of the world where a large conglomerate like
Delta Airlines has opened a call center, some will associate
it with exploitation, a new form of colonialism.

I wanted to put a stamp on the outsourcing world because
I am tired of it being used as this boogeyman by media
outlets, politicians, and economists who use it to advance
a particular agenda without a real understanding of its
nature.

The problem we have right now is that, as a society, we
talk about polarization as if it exists. It is a made-up idea
that slices people into different segments, markets, and
cultures and enforces the notion that there are enormous
differences between people. But there aren't.

If there is a constant thing that I have seen throughout my
career and many travels abroad, it's that we, as humans,
are extraordinarily similar in many ways. When you really
get down to the nuts and bolts of how we live our lives,

what we are motivated by, and what we are trying to do in this world, we are all very much the same. This is where the potential of an industry like outsourcing lies. It allows an individual to embody and tap into that role of being a global citizen.

I get it. The concept has been extensively distorted and there are two types of people commonly associated with it. We have pro-nationalists who are deeply proud of what they represent, be it a country or their town. I have known people who literally have rivaled each other based on the village they grew up in. Big shout out to Ireland for that. On the other hand, there are those who oppose it.

While it is certainly interesting to see people take pride in who they are and where they come from, it is equally important to appreciate the macro picture. This is where my core driving philosophy of positive nihilism comes into play, which recognizes the idea that we are on a rock that, through sheer infinitesimal chance, is habitable and spins around the sun in a void. We speculate about life on other planets, whether there's something else out there, heck, we even speculate whether this is all real.

There is a considerable number of people who believe we are already in the matrix, and if we take it at base value, the chance of our existence is indeed incredibly small. With that premise, should we not strive to be kind and more col-laborative with each other? Especially at this point in time, where I think one of the biggest problems we have is how we have approached stewardship of this planet and this assumption that infinite growth and expansion will always be possible.

But it doesn't take a mathematician to work out that infinite growth is impossible when your resources are finite. That's how a virus operates. It keeps going until it kills its host. Sure, it may also jump to a new host, but we're just going to kill the host if we keep going. It's not a long-term viable solution.

So, given that's been the driving force for our habitation on this planet, we need a decisive shift in how we interact with it. It will take a whole-scale effort. Being 'more environmentally friendly' or 'reducing fossil fuels' is too simplistic. Let's take the leather industry as an example. There was a whole movement advocating for the use of vegan leather. As it turns out, it was more toxic and less biodegradable for the planet than traditional leather. This is why we need to bring in nuance.

The way that we have marched towards progress has been generally positive. We have brought many, many humans out of poverty, and we should celebrate that. But it shouldn't cause us to turn a blind eye to the negative costs or externalities that have come with it. Unfortunately, we have never accounted for these costs in our business, economic, or social models. Now it's time to pay the bill and meaningfully create systems and solutions that can effectively tackle this and create positive change.

I am not religious in the conventional sense, but I was raised Catholic, and I still recall the Easter Service. It's a very long church service and grueling for a kid. One thing that stuck with me was there was always this man with a really magnanimous voice, who always told us about the story of Genesis. It says that "God created man to rule over this planet and to care for it." That's an important word there—"care." I believe that is something we have lost.

Regardless of your faith, whether you're an atheist or an agnostic, there is a common thread that connects us all the way back to mythology. We are on this planet, and we are on the top of the food chain, which means we have a duty not to abuse our position or exploit this privilege. It's easy to say, "Oh well, we're better than any other animal." But are we? If we go too far, look what happens. We have mass species extinction and untold damage to the earth's landscape.

Unfortunately, the alternative is not going to come from politicians. They are too short-term oriented and so focused on the next election cycle that they cannot operate with long-term perspectives knowing they could be out in a few years. In those horizons, it's not long at all. And if you look at existing companies that operate within one set of borders. That also won't work.

For us to get to any semblance of solutions that will work for us all, it has to be using the construction that has, ironically, driven the most change. The concept of money is something that we invented, and that sole invention has allowed us to multiply and distribute wealth. It has allowed us to get people out of poverty, and all with the right incentives.

Scientific breakthroughs in various industries throughout human history have all played a crucial role in achieving all these advancements. The outsourcing industry as it exists now is built on the backs of so many breakthroughs in video conferencing. It is, by and large, a service, and service is the tertiary level of the industry, even above manufacturing and agriculture. Services are the pinnacle, and if you can have all three of those in your nation, you're doing pretty well for yourself.

The harsh reality is, we have the option to do nothing and watch as the world hurtles toward destruction. And it will. Climate change and food insecurity are already playing a role, and it won't take much for those dominoes to start to fall, and we will witness large-scale migrations and wars that will ultimately lead us back to being protectionist and isolationist.

This cycle of events has happened many times throughout history. We need to remember that the trends of globalization that have existed basically since the end of the Second

World War are the exception to the rule rather than the rule. If we don't consciously find a way to stay connected on a global scale, then we are once again turning a blind eye to the challenges facing our planet.

The most basic reason to be concerned is that you live on this planet just as much as anyone else. Some countries might feel like they are slightly removed from an ongoing conflict or issue, but it will eventually affect them in some way. This is why it is so critical for us to unite as a species.

I understand that I'm asking people to unite under a banner that has been distorted and misused. Globalization has caused massive benefits to some while causing massive harm to others. Similarly, outsourcing has been praised for providing immense benefits to others while imposing significant disadvantages on others. What I would challenge you to think about is that these concepts, specifically outsourcing, aren't inherently good or bad. You can use it for good or evil purposes, the same way we have used money, which is not inherently good or evil. It merely magnifies the personality of the person who wields it.

A business owner who employs these practices is going to be resilient in the future. They are going to create companies that will unlock enormous wealth and good for them. But it is also going to play a role and cause shifts at a higher level. It is going to chart a path where more people can actually put their minds together to solve the biggest existential crisis that we have ever faced as a species. I am not claiming we will entirely solve this crisis, but we are certainly giving ourselves one hell of a shot to do it.

One of the things that frustrates me the most is when people use the collective as an excuse for individual bad behavior. It is common to see markets being blamed for negative costs, but markets are made up of people. Politicians will blame society, the electorate, or certain groups as reasons for not being able to carry out certain policies, but those groups are also made up of individuals.

We have constantly bickered at each other as a species. As a way to preserve our own tribe, we fault the outsider or follow the herd and consistently ignore the single greatest truth. Every human on this planet has enormous power and potential. If we can wield that correctly, unselfishly, and in a way that would actually do good for the planet, what a wonderful world that would be. This sheer lack of accountability and finger-pointing to blame others needs to stop.

It seems to me that we are still failing to realize our potential as a species.

We've always found ways to exploit and literally steal from each other. I know that more than anyone. I was born in a country that I shouldn't have been.

I'm a white man born at the bottom of the world where there was a pre-existing indigenous population of many hundreds, maybe even thousands, of different tribes and cultures that were obliterated because my ancestors decided to go around the world and be hostile to another group of people. At the same time, those same ancestors suffered at the hands of the English. While these roots are far back, they still have an impact on who I am today.

Throughout history, we have constantly prioritized our own gain at the expense of others. Economists would call this a zero-sum game, where there can be no real winner. You might win for a short time, but you will eventually lose. But why do we keep playing this way? We have repeatedly chosen a mindset of vindictiveness towards each other that has gone on for far too long, and it needs to stop.

It is a fair question to ask if it is even possible to change all this. This is where I will say, let's get away from the big breakthroughs. Instead, we should focus on fostering the right kind of intelligence, curiosity, and potential. Let's shift our attention back to the micro level, which is why I am passionate about outsourcing.

When I talk about the people I work with, I have worked with people right across the globe, a team of 15 people spread across four continents. Those people were able to have enriching lives because of the outsourcing model. It's just a small number of people, but the stories that have come out are truly inspiring.

If you look at what is in your domain as an individual who is really trying to make lives better, you have the power. This is something often faced by a leader. When I was a leader of a department, I knew I always had choices.

I could choose to blame all the external factors at play, the company, the CEO, economic forces, political and even legal environment, but I didn't because all the choices I make are mine. I may have been influenced by things outside of my own control, as we all are, but at the end of the day, it's me who gets to make the choice, and I need to own and take accountability for those choices.

When I look at each of my team members, I can honestly say that I have made each of their lives slightly better. For some, it could be much more than just slightly. It's a good feeling to know that and I hope that even when they no longer work with me, they will have been made richer for the experience and opportunity of having to work with me and for giving me a chance to serve them better as their leader. I hope I have been a positive change in their lives.

Funnily enough, I can make that point not just anecdotally and just to dispel the idea that I have delusions of grandeur; my team has been independently surveyed. If we look across the entire company that I have represented for the last several years, my department has had 100% satisfaction, and I am certainly not exaggerating those numbers.

I am sharing this with you because I refuse to believe that I am the only person capable of this. I'm a reasonably bright guy, but I am not a genius by any stretch of the imagination. I want to inspire others to create positive change in their own domains. That's what I want to see. Naturally, how I share my experience so it can inspire others starts from that mindset and by laying it all out from that structure.

Something impactful happened based on my little team of 15. Is it possible to spread that impact to companies and to business models? Ultimately, I want every human to take up this mantle. Because right now, for every one of me, there's JP Morgan, Coke Industries, Shell, Chevron, real estate conglomerates, and all types of industries that work against this potential for positive human change.

You might argue that it's not a fair ask because it's almost impossible to talk about this, let alone have people listen. But, you absolutely can. It's high time to recognize that we, as individuals, have allowed incentives to be manipulated against our best interests.

Start small. You can make an impact in your immediate surroundings and then gradually expand your efforts to make a difference. Something I read that I found very poignant is how in America, you have a handful of companies that raise the ire of the general populace. You have Blackrock, Vanguard, and State Street that are accused of owning 90+ percent of the Fortune 500. They own most of the big banks.

There are two ways to view this situation. The traditional view is that these are shadowy organizations pulling the strings, influencing politics and media. One thing that stuck with me though, is who do you think owns the majority of those companies? We do. Our investment funds, as a general populace, control these companies. That's an aspect that is somehow always overlooked.

It is quite common for people to quickly jump to the power structure, to get into the mindset that something is controlling them and their minds and making them do things they don't really want to do. Ironically, we initially owned these structures before they became industry behemoths. And I am not expecting a single individual to tackle these types of big institutions. They have very strong vested interests in the current structure of our society today, ensuring people continue to be unquestioning. It will require a collective effort, but you as an individual still hold an enormous power to have a positive impact and be a role model for others until we reach our goals.

Ultimately, if you got into business for the right reasons and have read this far into the book, you know it is not just about making a profit.

It's about the opportunity to be a light for other people.

That's why I do what I do.

It's exactly why I know many business owners do what they do.

And if we can continue that momentum, if we can show that level of care for one another, then maybe we can actually transfer that care to the world.

We have really come a long way as a species.

We need to remember that in the blink of an evolutionary cycle, we have gone from basically single-cell organisms to fish, to living underground like mole rats during the dinosaur era.

We burrowed underground and lived underground for a number of years, which is why we survived the great extinction event.

Then, there was the ape family, which was essentially food for saber-tooth tigers, cheetahs, and any other form of natural predator.

And we survived.

We weren't even the best human-like species in that era. It was the Neanderthals. They were the strongest and the most well-built for the different environments that we lived in. And yet we did it.

Homo sapiens prevailed because we used our brains. We utilized our cognitive abilities to do all sorts of wonderful things.

We started small.

We ceased to be nomadic and started working in agricultural areas to easy river valleys and expanded from there.

We created enormous civilizations all the way from China to the Romans to the Persian Empire.

We then spanned vast distances and came to the Americas, equipped with new technologies. We first harnessed the power of using horses and then advanced to trains.

At the turn of the 1900s, we invented the automobile and the airplane.

We literally challenged the natural dominion of birds, saying, "why should they be the only ones allowed to fly?"

We possess an enormous capacity for intelligence, a fact that should never be overlooked.

Yet, something happened along the way. Reflecting on a point in time when we weren't at the top of the food chain, still in the process of ascending toward it, and we were still operating within the boundaries of nature.

At some point, we decided to defy it, and it succeeded for a while until it didn't.

The black death of the 1300s was only a preview. Moving ahead to the 1800s, we witnessed the cholera outbreak in England.

Then we go to the colonialism era, when most indigenous

populations suffered at the hands of the Europeans not because of guns but because of smallpox, measles, and other diseases.

Despite the many advancements in modern medicine, we still face a fundamental crisis. The global pandemic of 2020 is a prime example. The exact efficiency we developed in getting around the world came back to bite us in a big way.

And this, I think, is the crux of our crisis.

We have such immense intellectual capacity that we have deluded ourselves into thinking we are bigger than nature, but we're not.

If you think it's been scary having a pandemic, having wildfires in my home of Australia, floods and earthquakes in Pakistan, and the war in Ukraine are all signs that there is going to be a hell lot more.

As I've said before, it's time to pay up.

That's the thing. We've lived our entire existence on borrowed time, and now we face a crucial, single choice to live or to die.

A younger Patrick would have told you there isn't even a choice, and we are already unconsciously or subconsciously choosing to die because humans just refuse to care.

However, upon closer look, many individuals do care, even

though it seems like a lot of them don't on the surface.

But that's when you go back to the individual. You find many similarities. This, I think, is one of the most powerful things that any person can do to approach, for better understanding, the larger issue of how we got so warped.

We started playing with the landscape of civilization, politics, and empires. Then it became far too big for any human to comprehend, and so it morphed into this inhuman structure of its own.

Let's take a step back and return to the human.

What drives a Homo sapien?

What you'll find is an individual who wants to provide for their family and wants their kids to live a better life than their own and live a life that they can be proud of.

Individuals want to make sure that they are providing water, shelter, personal fulfillment, belonging, and self-actualization if we take it all the way through Maslow's hierarchy.

We're not that different. At some core human level, we want the same things.

If I could, I would say to my former self, "you're wrong, there is still a choice. It's not a blind and senseless race toward death. We must choose between life and death and we must choose it with courage. It is not enough to leave this decision at a species level, it is crucial that we make the choice at an individual level. If enough of us make the right choice, we can set a course to correct our errors and ensure the survival of humanity."

The world will still be here whether we choose to live or die. But we won't if we choose the latter.

I don't know about you, but I would like to choose the former.

Return to the source, choose to outsource.

About the Author

Patrick Ward is the founder of NanoGlobals, an expert-led platform that helps mid-sized tech companies tap into global markets through remote hiring, offshoring, and international market expansion. He is also the VP of Marketing at Formula.Monks, the technology services division of Media.Monks, the unitary operating brand of S4 Capital. He has been featured in The New York Times, Ad Age, Fast Company, Morning Brew, HackerNoon, HuffPost, and Business Insider.

Patrick is an accomplished public speaker, as well as a guest lecturer on Executive Leadership at the University of North Carolina, and on AI and Technology Disruption at the University of Southern California. He also serves as a Board Director for the Sydney University Graduates Union of North America, a nonprofit organization.

He currently lives and works (sometimes remotely) in Los Angeles, California.

www.ingramcontent.com/pod-product-compliance
Lightning Source LLC
Chambersburg PA
CBHW041734200326
41518CB00020B/2588